Learning in Landscapes of Practice

D1572531

If the body of knowledge of a profession is a living landscape of practice, then our personal experience of learning can be thought of as a journey through this landscape. Within *Learning in Landscapes of Practice*, this metaphor is further developed in order to start an important conversation about the nature of practice knowledge, identity and the experience of practitioners and their learning. In doing so, this book is a pioneering and timely exploration of the future of professional development and higher education.

The book combines a strong theoretical perspective grounded in social learning theories with stories from a broad range of contributors who occupy different locations in their own landscapes of practice. These narratives locate the book within different contemporary concerns such as social media, multi-agency, multi-disciplinary and multi-national partnerships, and the integration of academic study and workplace practice.

Both scholarly, in the sense that it builds on prior research to extend and locate the concept of landscapes of practice, and practical because of the way in which it draws on multiple voices from different landscapes, *Learning in Landscapes of Practice* will be of particular relevance to people concerned with the design of professional or vocational learning. It will also be a valuable resource for students engaged in higher education courses with work-based elements.

Etienne Wenger-Trayner is an independent author, practitioner, and thought leader in the field of social learning theory and its application in various sectors.

Mark Fenton-O'Creevy is Associate Dean and Professor of Organizational Behaviour at the Open University Business School, UK. He is a National Teaching Fellow and a Senior Fellow of the Higher Education Academy.

Steven Hutchinson is Associate Dean in the Faculty of Education and Language Studies at the Open University. He has been a secondary school music teacher and Director of the Open University's programme in Initial Teacher Education.

Chris Kubiak originally trained as a community psychologist. He is currently a lecturer in the Faculty of Health and Social Care at the Open University.

Beverly Wenger-Trayner is a learning theorist and consultant working with systems conveners in complex settings.

Learning in Landscapes of Practice

Boundaries, identity,
and knowledgeability
in practice-based learning

Edited by Etienne Wenger-Trayner,
Mark Fenton-O'Creevy,
Steven Hutchinson, Chris Kubiak,
and Beverly Wenger-Trayner

Routledge
Taylor & Francis Group

LONDON AND NEW YORK

First published 2015
by Routledge
2 Park Square, Milton Park, Abingdon, Oxon OX14 4RN

and by Routledge
711 Third Avenue, New York, NY 10017

Routledge is an imprint of the Taylor & Francis Group, an informa business

British Library Cataloguing in Publication Data
A catalogue record for this book is available from the British Library

Library of Congress Cataloging in Publication Data
Learning in landscapes of practice : boundaries, identity, and knowledgeability in practice-based learning / edited by Etienne Wenger-Trayner, Mark Fenton-O'Creevy, Steven Hutchinson, Chris Kubiak, and Beverly Wenger-Trayner.
    pages cm
Includes bibliographical references and index.
ISBN 978-1-138-02218-8 (hardback)—ISBN 978-1-138-02219-5 (paperback)—ISBN 978-1-315-77712-2 (ebook) 1. Professional education.   2. Professional practice.   3. Professional learning communities.   4. Experiential learning. I. Wenger, Etienne, 1952–
LC1059.L42 2014
378'.013—dc23   2014002229

ISBN: 978-1-138-02218-8 (hbk)
ISBN: 978-1-138-02219-5 (pbk)
ISBN: 978-1-315-77712-2 (ebk)

Typeset in Galliard
by Keystroke, Station Road, Codsall, Wolverhampton

Contents

Contributors

Editorial team

Mark Fenton-O'Creevy is Professor of Organizational Behaviour at the Open University Business School, UK. He is a National Teaching Fellow and a Senior Fellow of the Higher Education Academy. He was formerly director of the Open University Practice Based Professional Learning Centre (PBPL), a UK Centre of Excellence for Teaching and Learning. His published research includes studies of the cross-national transfer of management practices within multi-national firms, the practice and learning of traders in investment banks and the role of emotion in financial decision-making.

Steven Hutchinson is Associate Dean for Learning and Teaching in the Faculty of Education and Language Studies at the Open University, UK. He worked as a secondary school music teacher and became Director of the Open University's programme in Initial Teacher Education, the PGCE, in 2000. He was a Principal of the Open University's Centre of Excellence in Practice Based Professional Learning (PBPL CETL) and directed the Centre from 2008 to 2009. Most recently, he established the TESS-India project that uses Open Education Resources to support teacher education in India. His research is focused on the relationship between academic practice and the school-based practice of teachers.

Chris Kubiak originally trained as a community psychologist. He is currently a lecturer in the Faculty of Health and Social Care at the Open University, UK. He has developed courses in areas such as youth justice, health and social care, and practice-based learning for support workers. His research work has included studies of online learning communities, school-based learning networks, practice-based education and the work-based learning of paraprofessionals in health and social care.

Beverly Wenger-Trayner is a learning theorist and consultant specializing in communities of practice and social learning systems. Her work with international organizations such as the Nuclear Threat Initiative, the International Labour Organization and the World Bank has given her substantial experience in coaching conveners in complex landscapes of practice. She has published articles about learning in internationally distributed communities and co-authored a popular toolkit on the emerging practice of social reporting.

Etienne Wenger-Trayner is an independent author, practitioner, and thought leader in the field of social learning theory and its application in various sectors, including business, government, international development, healthcare and education. He is best known for his work on communities of practice and has authored and co-authored seminal books on the topic. He pursues this inquiry through writing, consulting, keynotes, workshops, and visiting positions in universities.

Other contributors

Karen Appleby is a Principal Lecturer in Early Childhood within the Institute of Education at the University of Worcester. She is a Learning and Teaching Fellow at the University of Worcester and has a leadership role for student experience and achievement. She teaches across a variety of early childhood programmes. Previously she has worked as the Course Leader for the BA (Hons) Integrated Early Childhood Studies and HND in Early Childhood Studies and has coordinated the delivery of the Sector Endorsed Foundation Degree in Early Years in collaboration with eight partners. She has a particular interest in reflective practice and publishes work on this area of study.

Robert Bood is managing partner of FairSights, an international consulting company that supports organizations in creating better futures for the people they care about. He focuses on creating learning systems and practices in organizations to explore and anticipate the future, develop robust and distinctive strategies and create new, innovative business models on a continuous basis. He publishes and blogs regularly on these topics and is co-author of books on Communities of Practice and Network Learning (both in Dutch). Robert holds a PhD in Economics from the University of Groningen.

Lindsay Brigham has a healthcare background and has been a staff tutor in the Faculty of Health and Social Care with the Open University from the mid-1990s. The main focus of her role has been on teaching and learning and managing the delivery of health and social care education. She has published in the area of the social history of learning difficulties, emotional resilience in health workers and optimal organizational conditions for facilitating work-based learning and effective leadership and change.

Sheila Cameron has been involved in management education and development for over 30 years, as academic, tutor and coach, with a particular interest in how managers think and learn, and how the academic perspective sometimes fails to value what practising managers bring to the learning context. Publications include *The MBA Handbook* and *The Business Student's Handbook* (Pearson/FT, currently in 6th and 7th editions), and (with D. Price) *Business Research Methods* (The CIPD). She is currently working on a book on organizational behaviour.

Joanne Cashman, EdD, is the director of the IDEA Partnership, an investment by the Office of Special Education Programs (OSEP) at the US Department of Education (USDOE) and sponsored by the National Association of State Directors of Special Education (NASDSE). Joanne led the Partnership to pioneer Communities of Practice in education by crossing the boundaries of agency and role to seek solutions to persistent problems. The Partnership supports state decision-makers in convening CoPs that bring stakeholder networks into a learning partnership with the state agency. Joanne holds a Doctorate of Education from the George Washington University in Washington, DC (USA).

Marc Coenders, PhD, is an independent learning architect and advises organizations about the improvement of their learning capabilities. His passion is to facilitate networked learning and communities of practice. He likes to act as a bricoleur, designing professional learning trajectories along the way in close cooperation with members of a community. This is also a research approach by which disciplines are crossed, looking for unexpected connections and new perspectives.

Gráinne Conole is Professor of Learning Innovation at the University of Leicester. Her research interests include the use, integration and evaluation of Information and Communication Technologies and e-learning, and the impact of technologies on organizational change. She regularly blogs on www.e4innovation.com. She has successfully secured funding from the EU, HEFCE, ESRC, JISC and commercial sponsors. She was awarded an HEA National Teaching Fellowship in 2012. She has published and presented over 1,000 conference proceedings, workshops and articles, including the use and evaluation of learning technologies. She has recently published a Springer book entitled *Designing for Learning in an Open World*.

Patrice Cunniff Linehan, EdD, is a Senior Associate at the IDEA Partnership, a US Department of Education investment in stakeholder expertise. She joined the Partnership in 1999. Patrice supports national organizations as they convene learning partnerships around the issues they share, build an infrastructure for CoP development and chronicle the value created through their collaborations. Patrice holds a Doctorate of Education from the George Washington University in Washington, DC (USA).

Yannis Dimitriadis, PhD, is Professor of Telematics Engineering at the University of Valladolid, Spain. He is also coordinator of the GSIC/EMIC research group, since 1994, an inter-disciplinary team of more than 20 researchers from the fields of Telematics, Computer Science and Pedagogy. Besides his technical background, Prof. Dimitriadis' main research interest is the support of technology-enhanced learning activities, especially in computer-supported collaborative learning, through both conceptual and technological tools. His main contributions concern the field of learning design, interaction analysis and classroom orchestration.

Debbie Edwards has been a child-minder for 22 years. She completed a BA Early Years degree at the Open University. She is currently completing a 'Forest School Leader' qualification.

Gill Goodliff is Senior Lecturer and Head of Qualifications for Early Years at the Open University. A former social worker with young children and families, Gill has extensive experience of teaching early years practitioners in community-based contexts and colleges of Further Education and Higher Education. Her research interests include the professional development and identities of the early childhood workforce and young children's agency as meaning makers. Gill has a particular interest in understanding the spirituality of children under three years of age, which was the focus of her doctoral research.

Liz Hartnett is a university researcher, associate lecturer and tutor, a teacher, volunteer, wife, mother, stepmother, daughter and niece. As part of her research into relationships between public sector employees and IT consultants, she recognized the relevance of work on communities of practice, and thus came to the workshop on landscapes of practice. Liz is now researching how video-making and performance help science and technology teachers to identify barriers at knowledge boundaries, and how a participative video-making process can help students to breach those boundaries.

Richard Holti is Senior Lecturer at the Open University Business School. He has extensive experience of engaging with practitioners in manufacturing industry, construction and the NHS, using action research and leadership development to bring about innovation and new ways of organizing. He has researched and published on the changing nature of professional work, professional leadership and accountability. Before joining the OU in 2001 he worked for 18 years at the Tavistock Institute of Human Relations.

Sylvia Jones' most recent role has been as an English Language Advisor to the Ethiopian Ministry of Education advising on the development of curriculum for English language teacher education. Prior to this, she worked as a researcher in academic literacy and learning in Higher Education at the Open University, University of Leicester and University of West of England. She also has an extensive background in teacher education and curriculum development in the UK and Canada.

Maxine Kempster is a Programme Tutor with the Open University and a mental health nurse. She supports students with their practice-based learning on the university's nurse-training programme. During her nursing career, she specialized in working with older people and has a particular interest in dementia care.

Eilidh Mackay is currently Head of Teacher Development and an Advanced Skills Teacher in a secondary school in the South-East of England. She has worked in a variety of schools both in Scotland and England and has a keen interest in research in education. She has a MEd and is also a Chartered Teacher in Scotland.

Sue McKeogh is an Associate Lecturer with the Open University, tutoring across a range of work-based learning modules for practitioners working with children. She has a wealth of practice experience of working with children within the private, voluntary, and social care sectors, with a background in child-minding and youth work. She has completed doctoral research into how child-minders engage in reflective practice, and the development of professional identity.

Paul Mylrea is Director of Communications at the University of Cambridge. He has worked in public relations for more than a decade, including senior roles at Oxfam, Transport for London, the Department for International Development and the BBC. He began his career as a newspaper journalist and foreign correspondent for Reuters. He also works as an Associate Lecturer at the Open University Business School. He graduated with distinction in his own MBA from the OUBS and was given their MBA Student of the Year award in 2004. The Chartered Management Institute also named him 2008 London Chartered Manager of the Year.

Michael Reed is a Senior Lecturer at the Centre for Early Childhood, within the Institute of Education at the University of Worcester where he teaches on undergraduate and postgraduate courses. He has been part of course development and writing teams at the Open University and is an experienced author. He co-edited a number of books including *Reflective Practice in the Early Years* (2010), *Work Based Research in the Early Years* (2012) and most recently, *A Critical Companion to Early Childhood*. All are published by Sage.

Ellie Rees has exhibited extensively internationally including at Tate Modern, El Museo de Arte Contemporaneo, Venezuela and the Neuberger Museum of Art, New York. She has held many residencies in the UK, Europe, and America. Commissions include working for the Almeida Theatre, the Women's Library and English National Opera. Ellie's educational research focuses on the professional development of Fine Art students, and has been published by the UAL.

Mariola Rosser, EdD, is a Senior Associate at the IDEA Partnership, a US Department of Education investment in stakeholders' expertise. Mariola joined the Partnership in 2000. Mariola's role in the IDEA Partnership is to convene and support facilitators of mature Communities of Practice (CoPs) around school behavioural health and transition from school to college and career. Mariola also supports the grounding and initial development of new CoPs including autism, acquiring brain injury, and twice-exceptional students. Mariola holds a Doctorate of Education from the George Washington University in Washington, DC (USA).

Parm Sansoyer is a freelance Early Years Inspector with extensive experience in inspecting the full range of early years provision. She has worked directly with families and children in various contexts and as a therapist dealing with domestic violence, sexual abuse and mental health issues. She has co-authored a chapter on 'Quality improvement: integrated working', in a book published in 2012, *Implementing Quality Improvement and Change in the Early Years*.

Gill Scobie has worked in a number of inner city schools teaching English and Modern Languages and she has had a range of middle and senior management roles. She has been involved in initial teacher training in schools and universities, training teachers in the PGCE and GTP and Schools Direct programmes. She is now an education consultant and is involved in school improvement and inspection.

Alison Shreeve is Head of School, Design, Craft and Visual Arts at Buckinghamshire New University and previously the Director of Creative Learning in Practice Centre for Excellence in Teaching and Learning (CLIP CETL) at the University of the Arts London. She has a Masters in Art Education and a PhD in Educational Research. Research interests include the student and tutor experience in creative arts higher education. She has published articles in international journals and contributed to several books. She is associate editor of the journal *Art, Design and Communication in Higher Education* and a National Teaching Fellow.

Ann Smith has had considerable nursing and teaching experience having held a variety of posts in nursing practice, education and management. The main focus for her research has been on the nature and development of reflective practice. She has recently co-authored a book entitled *Compassion, Caring and Communication*.

Carla Solvason is a Senior Lecturer in the Centre for Early Childhood within the Institute of Education at the University of Worcester. She coordinates a teaching programme designed to encourage practice-based inquiry where students and settings work together. Prior to lecturing Carla worked as a teacher, a writer, a researcher and a consultant for schools looking to create communication-rich environments. She has published work relating to school culture, educational equality and social justice, collaborative working, ethicality and work-based research. Most recently she completed a text with Rosie Walker, *Success with your Early Years Research Project*, to be published by Sage.

Mary Thorpe is Professor of Educational Technology in the Open University, in the Institute of Educational Technology, where she was Director from 1995 to 2003. From 2007 to 2010 she was co-principal of the Practice-based Professional Learning Centre of Excellence in Teaching and Learning. She has extensive experience in course design, development and evaluation. She is currently Associate Director, Institute of Educational Technology, responsible for Quality Enhancement. She has published widely in the field of distance and online education, focusing recently on computer-mediated interaction, social networking, work-related online learning, and participation. Projects have been funded by the Andrew Mellon Foundation, by the National College for School Leadership, and by the UK JISC. She has recently led the development of a website for the professional development of social workers and care workers, http://peple.open.ac.uk.

Lisa Way is an experienced child-minder. She completed a BA Early Years degree at the Open University.

An invitation to a conversation

Steven Hutchinson, Mark Fenton-O'Creevy,
Gill Goodliff, Debbie Edwards, Liz Hartnett,
Richard Holti, Eilidh Mackay, Sue McKeogh,
Parm Sansoyer and Lisa Way

By the time Debbie and Lisa, two child-minders, reached the workshop venue they had turned back twice. Their worries about how they would engage with researchers, inspectors and teachers in their field, and a feeling that they wouldn't have much to contribute to the workshop process, were overwhelming. Perhaps it was our fault? As workshop organizers we obviously hadn't made it clear that it was precisely this set of concerns that made their contribution so important. Developing an understanding of their perspectives through the telling of 'boundary' stories was to be an important part of this event.

The workshop, held in Milton Keynes, England, brought together practitioners, researchers, Higher Education teachers and regulators from a variety of different fields to explore 'landscapes of professional practice'. They would do this through telling stories of their experiences at the boundaries of different practices. We hoped to explore what it means to live and work across boundaries between the different communities of practice that make up a professional landscape and to help us develop new thinking around learning in practice. We wanted to generate theoretical and practical insights into practice-based learning within a framework of social learning theory. We hoped that this would help us reflect on the changing nature of higher education and professional development.

This book and the workshop had their origins in a conversation about learning between Etienne Wenger[1] and the Practice Based Professional Learning Centre at the Open University, in the UK. In his 1998 book *Communities of Practice: Learning, meaning and identity* (Wenger, 1998) Etienne started with the question 'So, what if we adopted a different perspective, one that placed learning in the context of our lived experience?'. Building on his earlier work with Jean Lave, Etienne set out a highly influential account of social learning, which placed participation in communities of practice at the heart of a social learning theory. This book has been an important influence on much recent work on learning. Google Scholar identifies more than 26,000 citations of the work in the 14 years since its publication.

This focus on communities of practice has been highly productive but, in our view, has led at times to too great a focus on single communities and on the apprenticeship trajectory from periphery to heart of the community of practice.

In some circles, it has become, for example, commonplace for university educators to talk in terms of creating communities of practice for their students, or of bringing them into an academic community of practice. This usefully highlights the notion of learning as participation in practice, but obscures the multiple communities to which students belong and the likelihood that their eventual destinations lie outside the academic community.

Also in Wenger's 1998 book was a broader idea that we thought deserved fuller exploration, that of landscapes of practice which consist of many different communities of practice and the boundaries between them. The metaphor of a landscape ensures that we pay attention to boundaries, to our multimembership in different communities and to the challenges we face as our personal trajectories take us through multiple communities.

The workshop and writing of this book also has its origins in the work of the Centre for Practice-Based Professional Learning. The centre was a UK-government-funded centre for excellence in teaching and learning at the Open University between 2005 and 2010. Those of us who led and worked at this centre were engaged in exploring ways of improving the learning of practitioners in fields such as teaching, nursing, social work, management and accounting. In this workshop our goal was to look at those fields as landscapes of practice and to focus on the learning that goes on (or fails to go on) at the boundaries between the different communities of practice within them. Participants in this workshop have joined us as co-authors in chapters of this book. By working with a wide range of people from different practice contexts we have tried to ensure the ideas in the book can be productive in different settings.

Let us return to that workshop which Debbie and Lisa had been so nervous about joining. To introduce themselves, participants told their own professional stories, moving around a metaphorical professional landscape on the venue floor. 'Lily pads' each represented a different facet of professional practice within that landscape. A person's trajectory across the lily pads served as a trigger for a story about their experiences as practitioners, researchers, academics, regulators or inspectors in their respective fields. Participants moved from pad to pad as they described the journeys they had undertaken. Sometimes they straddled different pads as they shared stories of how they played multiple roles. It became clear that each person's journey was more complex than might appear on the surface.

Out of this activity we coalesced into different groups to explore our experiences in more depth. Some groups formed around particular professional landscapes. For example one group consisted of child minders, university lecturers for 'early years' practitioners and an inspector from the body responsible for oversight of childcare provision. Others coalesced around common experiences, such as the group who came together to discuss experiences of failure in transitions from one community of practice to another. Each group crafted stories to engage the wider group in some of the tensions of a journey through a particular landscape. Some were narrative accounts of lived experience. Others were fictional situations or mini-dramas to convey important elements of the experience.

The next chapter introduces some theory that underpins our understanding of these journeys through landscapes of practice. But first we will share some of the stories and role-plays crafted by the groups. We use these stories to highlight some of the issues we will address later in the book, but also to make clear that the phenomena with which this book is concerned are not exotic or rare, but part of the texture of our everyday experience.

A parents' consultation evening

One group at the workshop explored unsatisfactory experiences of parents' consultation evenings at school. Two parents of school-age children and a teacher shared unhappy experiences of these evenings. Their light-hearted and fictional play led to a discussion about how to bring together their different practices as teachers and parents.

The Year 10 parents' evening – an encounter between practitioners

Teachers heave a collective sigh in the run-up to a parental meeting evening, as it signals a long day and an evening stolen. Parents resent having to rush to school from work, often having to leave early or even take holiday to ensure they make the event on time.

To set the scene, this experience takes place in the school hall generally – scuffed, dirty and badly lit. Teachers sit with their backs to the wall (literally!) and parents press in on them from the other side of the table. Queues form as parents jostle and strive to maintain their hectic schedule of ten minutes with as many teachers as they can. Some teachers hide behind their laptop and refer to it regularly as though it somehow will provide the answer to a question. Some teachers can be seen checking their watches as if they are wishing the time away while others engage with the parents and their children, welcoming them with a smile and encouragement. There is the pupil sat between two parents, being berated by all parties. There is the pupil lapping up the many positive comments from the teacher. There is the pupil who would rather be playing football.

The parents are diverse. They can range from cooperative, well-meaning and realistic to judgemental, harsh and even confrontational.

Time pressure is ever present – clocks watched and watches adhered to. For some, minutes are endured and counted and wished away. Senior management 'meet and greet' at the main entrance and keep a careful eye on proceedings – checking everyone in and out – parents and teachers alike.

The evening tails off and everyone breathes a collective sigh of relief. Parents, pupils and teachers almost congratulate themselves on having endured the evening and some can even be heard exclaiming that it was a good experience 'really'.

The cast of characters and their preoccupations as practitioners

Ms Webber is senior subject teacher (Modern Foreign Languages), on duty this evening as a teacher of German to an examination group. She works at Comfortown High School, a state secondary school that parents in the locality regard as the state

---

sector school of choice, because of its excellent exam results and standing in local and national school rankings. Ms Webber has a wide range of classroom teaching strategies and techniques at her disposal, and also prides herself on accurately assessing the potential of students and deciding the right degree to which to push each student to improve their grade. This kind of issue is coming more sharply into focus for students, hopefully providing the basis for moving on to higher level study. But the continued good reputation of the school – and to an extent of Ms Webber – will depend above all on the proportion of students who achieve passes at grade C or above. The Principal will also be taking an interest in how many of the very highest grades Ms Webber produces.

Amy is a student in Ms Webber's class who chose to do German as a third language because she liked her French teacher and her 'fun' style of teaching, and the Languages Department was keen to enrol as many students as possible to do a second language in addition to French. The Comfortown High School Languages Department does not want to go the way of many other departments in secondary school where many students decide not to study languages because they are 'too difficult'. Studying two languages, however, doubles the vocabulary lists that Amy has to contend with. And she's also busy discovering that there is considerable 'fun' to be had outside of school, and that the rules at home which she has hitherto mostly observed – being home for 9pm curfew, doing chores round the house, doing homework before you get TV, for example – are in fact quite easy to flout. Her parents don't know what to do when she simply doesn't comply, and are completely powerless when she comes home after midnight having spent the evening 'hanging' with her mates in the local park, on occasion fuelled by a bottle of vodka that her friend Emily can nick from her Dad's study.

David is a hard-working professional – he is a manager in the voluntary sector, although his first degree was in German. He is the committed father of Amy, and has come to the parents' evening with Amy, to spend the usual 10 minutes with each of her subject teachers. His wife Kathleen couldn't make it because she has a clash with a meeting of a community pressure group where she has a leading role. David is concerned at the impact that Amy's current 'I'll do what I want' approach is having on her school work, and that there should be sanctions at school when she doesn't do her homework. Surely the school can do its bit to bring her back in touch with the realities of life? It shouldn't be down to him and Kathleen to battle on their own with Amy's foolishness and lack of responsibility.

The meeting

Ms Webber begins the ten-minute time slot scheduled for Amy and her Dad with a formal welcome for David and cheery 'Hi' to Amy. Amy has been sitting sullenly beside her Dad whilst they have been waiting outside Ms Webber's room, but suddenly lights up with a beautiful smile and gives Ms Webber an obscure teenage hand salute: 'Hi Miss'.

Ms Webber then puts a piece of paper in front of the parent–student pair, showing the target grade at the beginning of the year, current achievement, a revised target for the end of the year and a score for effort in class and in homework. Amy's original target was a B, but she is now performing at C level. Ms Webber thinks that a B is still on the cards. Amy's classroom effort is 'good', and her homework is 'satisfactory'. All in all, says Ms Webber, she has no real concerns about Amy, although she could try a little harder all round. As she finishes speaking, Ms Webber smiles again at Amy, and Amy does her curious salute again with a fleeting smile, indicating that she has taken in the need to perform a little better, and that she also feels that her general teenage cool and dignity are intact. 'No real concerns' means she's doing fine, so Dad can't complain about that, can he?

David finds himself getting angrier and angrier as Ms Webber is speaking. Doesn't she realize that Amy has an excellent brain and could easily be getting A's? Surely her role is to inspire and motivate Amy, not let her get away with lazing around and evading her responsibilities in life? And doesn't she realize that Amy isn't doing any homework? How can anyone learn a language without regular study of vocabulary? Or don't they have to do any real language learning any more?

He manages to stem his inner flow of indignation sufficiently to focus on one issue. Homework!

'I'm really concerned that Amy doesn't seem to be doing German homework very much at all. I keep asking her if she has any, and she always tells me "No, Miss didn't give us any this week", or "I've done it". Surely you're picking up on whether she does the homework?' Amy rolls her eyes, largely for the benefit of Ms Webber.

Ms Webber begins to respond 'Well, I don't have time to check or mark all the homework . . .' But Amy realizes she can take the initiative here very nicely. She turns to her Dad, all of a sudden very grown up. 'Dad, you always say you'll help me with my German, because you know, you're just so good at it, but then you never have time to actually help me. Your work is always more important.' David is hooked. 'What do you mean? I offered to help you just last weekend.' 'Yes, but you said you could only do it on Sunday morning, and Hullo, I'm a teenager, I sleep on Sunday mornings.' 'Well if you weren't running round with your idiot friends doing God knows what in the small hours of the morning, you might be able to get up.'

It's Ms Webber's turn to roll her eyes now, albeit discreetly, as typical family row variant 3a seems to be gathering force in front of her. She spots a chance to deflect the discussion away from the homework issue. 'So Amy's out late without supervision? That can't be good for her schoolwork. And I'm sure you can find a convenient arrangement for the two of you to work on Amy's homework.' And then the way forward clarified: 'Of course you have to remember that homework is precisely that: **home** work. I'm responsible for the **school** work . . .'

This is, perhaps, a story that is recognizable to most teachers and many parents. But most teachers and parents don't have the time or space to talk about how frustrating these exchanges can be. The encounter concerns different kinds of practice: the practices of a school teacher, parenting practices and the learning practices of a young person. As we will argue later in the book, boundary encounters between different practices can be important opportunities for learning but also bring significant challenges. Through this role-play the group was able to discuss what happens when communication across the boundary breaks down.

In their story, the teacher and parent fail to communicate effectively across the boundary between them. As our workshop progressed, the question this group addressed shifted from 'what happens in such meetings?' to 'what would it take to convene an encounter in which parents, pupils and teachers develop a fuller understanding of what needs to happen to support student learning?'

Liz's story focuses on her experiences with a housing officer[2] as she attempts to support her aunt in a difficult life transition.

Liz's story: an encounter with a housing officer

My aged aunt had been getting confused and forgetful, so I had taken out and registered a legal power of attorney for her property and affairs, but the first time I had to do anything was when I was called to a meeting with her, my father and a district council housing officer. My aunt needed to move from her own home to sheltered accommodation.

When I arrived to meet with a couple of frail octogenarians, a friend who'd been helping and the housing officer, I could immediately sense the tension. I had expected a discussion and exchange of information. However, I'd been given the wrong brief as to the purpose of the meeting, and the housing officer had a different agenda. She expected my aunt to sign papers and take the keys to the flat, which meant she would have to pay rent from the following Monday. This was a surprise as we hadn't expected her to move so quickly and we simply weren't ready to just pack up and go.

Regulations required that the officer read papers to us, and have my aunt sign in the next hour, but these regulations would not allow us copies of the papers in advance, not even of the tenancy agreement, though we could have a copy after it was signed. The officer spoke so loud that my aunt complained it hurt her ears and read the papers so quickly that we could not understand. We had limited time, because the officer had to leave at 3 o'clock. Eventually, we refused to sign, allowed the officer to leave on time and rearranged the meeting for another day. We came out feeling as if my aunt was being bulldozed into signing without having the information she needed. We were all bruised by the encounter.

Things were different at the next meeting. The housing officer had brought reinforcements in the form of her line manager. I shared information about myself, the officials gave me their contact details, then more calmly explained information that my aunt needed to make a decision. I'd done the homework needed to help her make that decision and could share it with the officials. Everyone left with smiles.

For those of us who have had poor experiences at the hands of professionals this story may be a familiar one. A lack of information, poor communication and competing agendas characterize this difficult encounter. Liz considers herself a competent person in her everyday life, but she faced the experience of being rendered incompetent by her unfamiliarity with the way in which the housing process was conducted. The housing officer took refuge in formal practices such as reading out the rental agreement, rather than engaging with the understanding Liz and her aunt had developed of the management of her aunt's care needs.

In these kinds of encounters between professional practitioners and service users, formalized practices can become a way of avoiding engaging with the complexity of users' lives and needs. This particular housing officer demonstrated a narrow understanding of her role. By contrast the second encounter involved a more experienced professional who understood the wider context in which their role was situated and the need to engage across the boundary between housing rules and practices and user needs. Offering opportunities for explanation, setting out the constraints under which each is operating, understanding more about the perspectives of others, seeing Liz and her relatives and friends as experts in the needs of her aunt, entering into a process of negotiation, eventually yielded a more satisfactory outcome.

The child-minders: the story of an inspection

We return now to the child-minders who began our chapter. They eventually made it to the workshop and ended up working with an early years inspector and a university lecturer who were also participating in the workshop. Between them they decided to reflect on the boundaries between their roles and to explore the act of inspection as a boundary experience. From their reflections they produced a mini-play they performed for the other workshop participants.

Coming together in this way was an unusual form of professional development for both the child-minders and the inspector. In England the inspectorate is responsible for the registration and regulation of care and educational provision for young children. Child-minders are home-based carers for young children who are regularly inspected to ensure standards are met. The results of inspection can determine whether or not the child-minder can continue to provide a service. Usually inspectors and child-minders only meet during an inspection event. They made these comments after the workshop:

> The workshop enabled us to see the inspector as a person . . . in some ways [they are] viewed as a 'policeman' – their role is to find fault and 'knock them down'. It was 'unusual to be having a coffee with an inspector!' (Debbie and Lisa – child-minders)

> [It] created neutral ground and allowed me the opportunity to interact and participate with child-minders for the first time in my twelve years of inspecting early years provision . . . (Parm – Inspector)

For both sets of participants, just meeting each other on neutral ground and having time to talk about their histories and their roles, was a valuable learning experience. The conversations they had, and the story they tell, are a vivid illustration of how new insights can be gained by bringing together people from different positions in the landscape to negotiate a particular practice without the dynamics associated with the inspector's more powerful position.

Together they scripted a light-hearted, humorous role-play (which they videoed) depicting a typical inspection reversing their roles so the inspector played the child-minder and the child-minder the inspector. The second child-minder played the off-screen, inner voice of both the inspector and the child-minder and through their voices revealed some of the 'behind the scenes' thoughts that both a child-minder and an inspector might have during an inspection.

CHILD-MINDER: Hello

CHILD-MINDER INNER VOICE: Oh s**t trust it to be today

INSPECTOR: Hello my name is Joanne Smith, I've come to do your Inspection today

INSPECTOR INNER VOICE: (Sarcastically) You're obviously pleased to see me

CHILD-MINDER: Come in and meet the children

CHILD-MINDER INNER VOICE: But don't look at the mess in the kitchen

INSPECTOR: Hello and what's your name?

INSPECTOR INNER VOICE: Oh isn't she cute (the child), but don't pay her too much attention I don't want to get in trouble for favouritism.

CHILD-MINDER: Would you like to see my paperwork?

CHILD-MINDER INNER VOICE: I was up all night doing that so you had better give me an outstanding!

INSPECTOR: Ok thank you!

INSPECTOR INNER VOICE: Oh my gosh does she expect me to look through all this? I'll be here all day!

INSPECTOR: Carry on with the children and do what you would normally do with them.

INSPECTOR INNER VOICE: As long as that's not watching daytime television with your feet up!

CHILD-MINDER: OK that's fine we're busy playing with dough

CHILD-MINDER INNER VOICE: How am I supposed to be doing that with you watching me like a hawk?

CHILD-MINDER: Ooh well done!

CHILD-MINDER INNER VOICE: Oh kids please be good! Don't play up!

CHILD-MINDER: Oh no Joe you know we need to share – please give it back.

CHILD-MINDER INNER VOICE: Oh good God, please STOP staring and scribbling in that bloody notepad!!

INSPECTOR INNER VOICE: She's playing lovely with the children . . . I've got some really good observations here. This inspection shouldn't take long

CHILD-MINDER: Oh no Joe, you know we don't do that here!

CHILD-MINDER INNER VOICE: Oh no I'm going to get done for child abuse now!

INSPECTOR INNER VOICE: She dealt with that really well and the children respond to her easily.

INSPECTOR: Just looking through your policies – do you have one for child protection?

CHILD-MINDER INNER VOICE: That's it, I might as well give up now, it's all going downhill from here.

Outwardly, this small drama reflects the high stakes involved in this kind of inspection, but the inner voices show an attempt by the group to reveal what people were really thinking. The inspector, who used to be a child-minder, is unable to express her professional interest as it might imply favouritism. At times she seems overwhelmed.

While the inspector looks for the positive, the child-minder, conscious of the impact that this inspection might have on her livelihood, is concerned that her behaviour might be perceived negatively.

Taking part in this workshop activity proved to be a motivating experience for both the child-minders and for the inspector. None of the participants had worked in this way before and they all note after the workshop that the experience has changed their views of themselves and the way they carry out their practice. By exploring their wider joint purpose in the landscape of childcare practice, the inspector feels that she became more understanding and supportive in the way that she provides feedback. One of the child-minders sought career advancement shortly after the workshop.

The stories in this chapter illustrate just how common these encounters are between different practices, accountabilities and understandings. They illustrate how exploring different practices in the landscape can be important opportunities for learning. We use other stories later in the book to investigate the implications of a 'landscapes of practice' perspective in more detail. In the next chapter, Etienne and Beverly develop some important ideas which will underpin this exploration.

Notes

1. Now Etienne Wenger-Trayner.
2. Local authority housing officers manage and allocate rental accommodation owned by the local government. This housing stock usually supports social objectives and the housing officers typically have a role in assessing and supporting the needs of tenants.

References

Wenger, E. (1998). *Communities of Practice. Learning, Meaning and Identity.* Cambridge: Cambridge University Press.

Part I

Theory

In this section of the book, which consists of just one chapter, we introduce some social learning theory which provides a foundation for our later discussions.

Chapter 1

Learning in a landscape of practice

A framework

Etienne Wenger-Trayner
and Beverly Wenger-Trayner

One day we were sitting in the office of a friend who is a lawyer. Pointing to a collection of volumes on her bookshelf she informed us that this was the 'body of knowledge' of her profession. It was an impressive series of thick books. Later on, we both agreed we were glad not to be lawyers, not to be held accountable to all that knowledge. While we understood what she meant, we agreed that this expression 'body of knowledge' was a convenient but possibly misleading short-hand. For social learning theorists like us the 'body' of knowledge of a profession is not just contained in a set of books. As important as the books undoubtedly are, they are only part of the story. They are too dead to constitute the full body of a living practice. From a social perspective we see the real 'body of knowledge' as a community of people who contribute to the continued vitality, application, and evolution of the practice.[1]

For professional occupations, however, the social body of knowledge is not a single community of practice. In this chapter we argue that the 'body of know-ledge' of a profession is best understood as a 'landscape of practice' consisting of a complex system of communities of practice and the boundaries between them. Developing the metaphor of a landscape of practice, first introduced in *Communities of Practice: Learning, Meaning and Identity* (Wenger, 1998), pro-vides a broad social perspective on professional learning, and learning more gener-ally. To account for the complex relations that people build across the landscape, we introduce the concept of knowledgeability. Whereas we use competence to describe the dimension of knowing negotiated and defined within a single com-munity of practice, knowledgeability manifests in a person's relations to a multi-plicity of practices across the landscape. In these relations identification may involve little or no accountability to actual competence. Yet these practices may be just as significant in constituting an identity of knowledgeability, if identification is understood as something that is modulated across the whole landscape.

Knowing in practice: regimes of competence

Being practicing members in good standing of a respected community of practice is a key reason why practitioners of any occupation deserve our patronage.

If your doctor informed you that he had seen many patients in the last twenty years, but had not talked to any colleague, read any new article, or participated in any conference, you may question whether he was really qualified to deal with your health. Conversely, if he told you that he had read endless articles, but not treated any patients, you would have the same question about his legitimacy. You trust practitioners like your doctor to help you both for their experience and personal characteristics, and also because their actions reflect a competence defined by their community. Connection, engagement, status, and legitimacy in that community are all part of what makes someone a trustworthy practitioner.

One could in fact define a responsible practitioner as someone whose experience in providing a service reflects the current competence of a community. In this sense, the community's social negotiation of what constitutes competence results in a regime of competence: membership in good standing entails accountability to that competence. The importance of accountability to such a regime can be appreciated in the example of a malpractice lawsuit against a doctor. The fact that a patient died, however regrettable, is not in itself an indictment of the doctor; it is a piece of data. To adjudicate the case, a judge has to bring other members of this doctor's community to testify whether their accused colleague has been competent in applying the most current practice of the community. It is this mix of personal experience and accountability to the regime of competence of a respected community that assures professional standing and constitutes someone's identity as a practitioner.

In the sense used here, competence includes a social dimension. Even as manifested by individuals, competence is not merely an individual characteristic. It is something that is recognizable as competence by members of a community of practice.

A regime of competence is not static, however. It shapes personal experience but can also be shaped by it. It is both stable and shifting as it lives in the dynamic between individuals' experience of it and the community's definition of it. Indeed, competence and experience are not a mere mirror-image of each other. They are in dynamic interplay. Members of a community have their own experience of practice, which may reflect, ignore, or challenge the community's current regime of competence. Learning in a community of practice is a claim to competence: it entails a process of alignment and realignment between competence and personal experience, which can go both ways. When newcomers are entering a community, it is mostly the regime of competence that is pulling and transforming their experience – until their experience reflects the competence of the community. This is what happens in apprenticeship, for instance. Conversely, experience can also pull, challenge, and transform the community's regime of competence. A member can find a new solution to a problem and attempt to convince the community it is better than existing practice. The experience of the physician whose patient died may challenge the community into reconsidering its practice. Any new experience that does not quite fit the regime of competence may cause the community to inspect and renegotiate its definition of competence. Or not. A challenge or a claim to competence may be refused by the community; a newcomer may be marginalized; a dissertation turned down; a new idea dismissed. Acceptance or resistance may be well founded, groundless, or even politically motivated. However derived, it remains potentially contestable. The power to define competence is at stake. Learning as a social process always involves these issues of power.

This dynamic interplay of experience and competence is why active engagement in a community of practice is so important for someone to become and remain current as a practitioner in a domain. For those who receive their services, reliable, up-to-date practitioners embody the evolving regime of competence of their community.

A body of knowledge as a landscape of practice

The notion of a single community of practice misses the complexity of most 'bodies of knowledge.' Professional occupations, and even most non-professional endeavors, are constituted by a complex landscape of different communities of practice – involved not only in practicing the occupation, but also in research, teaching, management, regulation, associations, and many other relevant dimensions.[2] All these practices have their own histories, domains, and regimes of competence.[3] The composition of such a landscape is dynamic as communities arise and disappear, evolve, merge, split, compete with or complement each other, ignore or engage the other. Landscapes of practice are coming into focus as globalization, travel, and new technologies expand our horizons and open up potential connections to various locations in the landscape.

To understand how a landscape of practice constitutes a complex 'social body of knowledge,' it is useful to consider some key characteristics.

The landscape is political: the power dynamics of practice

Various practices have differential abilities to influence the landscape through the legitimacy of their discourse, the legal enforcement of their views, or their control over resources. Regulators produce national policies and verify compliance with auditing practices. Theorists devise 'discourses of truth' (Foucault, 1970) and abstract models that attempt to shape how people talk about practice. Researchers seek evidence for what works in the hope that their findings will direct practice. Teachers impart the right curriculum and grant degrees to those who seem to get it. Managers design work systems, distribute budgets, give orders, and set local policies. All these practices represent attempts to colonize the field of practice in various ways. And practitioners sometimes comply with mandates and demands, and sometimes shrug it all off as too disconnected to be relevant. Sometimes they even create an appearance of compliance while doing their own thing.

In this sense the landscape of practice is political. The power dynamics of defining competence inherent in communities of practice have a counterpart among practices. A landscape consists of competing voices and competing claims to knowledge, including voices that are silenced by the claim to knowledge of others. This creates knowledge hierarchies among practices. In such a political landscape, there is no guarantee that a successful claim to competence inside a community will translate into a claim to 'knowledge' beyond the community where it is effective. Whether the competence of a community is recognized as knowledge depends on its position in the politics of the landscape.

The landscape is flat: the local nature of practice

A more traditional view of knowledge suggests that knowledge flows from practices that produce it to practices that receive it: whether it is top-down, north–south, or center–periphery; and at times it seems as though communities even conspire to keep it that way. A colleague was doing a detailed ethnographic study in a hospital. She observed a clear hierarchy of practices. For instance, she said that when a group of nurses have an idea about what to do about a patient, they 'do this little dance' (her expression with a corresponding hand gesture) to make sure that it looks as though the idea came from the doctor.

The nurses' story illustrates the pervasive power of a 'hierarchy of knowledge'; but it also suggests that the hierarchical view misses something important. Even if they conspired to make it invisible, the nurses had their own understanding of the patient, which reflected their perspective and experience. The hierarchy was real enough, but it masked a more complex reality.

In a landscape, all practices are practices. Regulation, management, and research are practices too, with their own local regimes of competence, just like frontline work. In this complex system, no practice can claim to contain or represent the whole, even if, like policy-makers, managers, or development agencies, they have the power or resources to influence large regions of the landscape with their perspective. Scale is not free. Collecting data for research, extracting measurements for management, or using financial rewards for compliance can achieve scale, but it loses some of the texture of the experience of practice itself. Therefore, all practices in the landscape have a fundamental 'locality.'

There is an internal logic to any practice because it is the production of the community that engages in it. A mandate or a set of standards may give rise to a practice, but they do not produce the practice; the practitioners do. It is their practice even if it is produced in compliant response to a mandate. Similarly, regulations inform practice in the sense that they become an influential element of judgment; but regulations do not produce practice: even a practice of strict compliance is produced by the practitioners.

That one practice has more power than another in the landscape does not mean that it 'subsumes' the other. In other words one practice cannot have such control over another that it replaces the internal logic and local claim to knowledge of that other practice; the knowledge of one practice is never merely implemented in another. Practices in a landscape inform and influence each other. For instance, a detailed national curriculum with minute prescriptions and regular inspections will definitely influence the practice of teachers. Such radical combination of curriculum design and enforcement may silence the perspectives of teachers or render the competence of their practice invisible or irrelevant. It may even sap their enthusiasm and engender a practice of cynicism and passive resistance as a response. But engendering such a response is not the same thing as one practice subsuming another. Engagement in lived practice is too complex and dynamic to be a mere implementation of prescription or the simple application of research. There is local knowing in each practice, whether or not this local knowing is recognized as knowledge in the broader landscape. Without denying the reality of the power dynamics among practices, there is a sense in which the landscape is flat. Relations among practices are at once epistemologically flat, politically unequal, and potentially contestable.

The landscape is diverse: boundaries of practice

If a practice could subsume another, then the boundary between them would be unproblematic. Practitioners would simply implement regulations, mandates, and evidence-based prescriptions. But meaning is produced in each practice. Because this makes mere subsumption impossible, relationships between practices are always a matter of negotiating their boundary. Without subsumption, the boundaries between practices are never unproblematic, in the sense that they always involve the negotiation of how the competence of a community of practice becomes relevant (or not) to that of another.

Boundaries of practice are unavoidable. A practice of any depth requires a sustained history of social learning, and this creates a boundary with those who do not share this history. Boundaries of practice are not necessarily formally marked, but they are unmistakable. Spend your lunch break with a group of computer geeks and you know what a boundary of practice is: you can't make sense of what they are talking about or why they are so passionate in talking about it. You might as well have landed on another planet.

Because of the lack of shared history, boundaries are places of potential misunderstanding and confusion arising from different regimes of competence, commitments, values, repertoires, and perspectives. In this sense, practices are like mini-cultures. Even common words and objects are not guaranteed to have continuity of meaning across a boundary. And the boundaries between the practices involved are not necessarily peaceful or collaborative. What researchers find, what regulators dictate, what management mandates, what international development agencies try to make happen, what clients expect, and what practitioners end up deciding, all these attempts to colonize moments of practice can be in conflict – hidden or open.

At the same time, boundaries hold potential for unexpected learning. The meetings of perspectives can be rich in new insights, radical innovations, and great progress. The name of a discipline like psycho-neuro-immunology reflects its birth at the boundaries between practices. Engaging at boundaries can expand what a community sees as important or even core to its practice. Of course new insights are not guaranteed and the likelihood of irrelevance makes engagement at the boundaries a potential waste of time and effort. Indeed, competence is less well defined at boundaries. As a consequence, the innovation potential is greater, but so is the risk of wasting time or getting lost.

Crossing boundaries, boundary encounters, and boundary partnerships are necessary for the integration of a landscape of practice. In a complex landscape in which no practice simply subsumes another, boundaries of practice are interesting places. Crossing a boundary always involves the question of how the perspective of one practice is relevant to that of another. It is connecting two forms of competence whose claim to knowledge may or may not be compatible. Therefore, boundary crossing and boundary encounters are crucial aspects of living in a landscape of practice.

Boundaries as learning assets

Pedagogically it might be tempting to hide the importance of boundaries under the guise of a reified, self-standing curriculum, that is, to make it seem as though what is taught in a course represents a body of knowledge unproblematically applicable to practice. Such an approach certainly simplifies teaching as well as testing.[4] Rather than hiding boundaries under an illusion of seamless applicability across contexts, it is better to focus on boundaries as learning assets. Such an approach confronts explicitly the problematic nature of boundary crossing and the potential tensions or conflicts between practices as sources of accountability. It does so in order to bring out the potential of boundary encounters to generate new insights. This focus on boundary encounters suggests the following questions:

- What kind of boundary activity, joint project, visit, mutual storytelling or learning partnership can serve as a productive encounter for negotiating and exploring a boundary?
- How can boundaries be used systematically to trigger a reflection process about the practices on either side?
- What kind of boundary objects and activities can support this boundary-oriented pedagogy and create points of focus for engaging multiple perspectives?
- Who can act as brokers to articulate regimes of competence across boundaries?

The principle is to systematically make boundaries a learning focus rather than assuming or seeking an unproblematic applicability of knowledge across practices. Bringing together multiple voices that reflect the structure of the landscape is crucial in several respects. First, it helps people locate themselves in the landscape and its constitution through the politics of knowledge. Done sensitively it can enhance the potential for reflexivity in the practices involved: it is difficult for communities of practice to be deeply reflective unless they engage with the perspective of other practices. Combining multiple voices can produce a two-way critical stance through a mutual process of critique and engagement in reflection. For instance, a practitioner taking a university course can use theory as a critical stance toward practice; and then conversely use practice as a critical stance toward theory. Another example is the problem of using research as evidence base: how does evidence translate into practice without robbing practice of its own engaged logic, what kind of boundary processes would facilitate this translation, and what kind of local reflective communities can help research be used productively in practice? This high-lights the importance of intentional moments of boundary crossing and boundary encounter that enable first-hand experience of the potential pitfalls, misunderstandings, and innovative opportunities of relevant boundaries.

Knowledgeability in a landscape of practice

We cannot be competent in all the practices in a landscape, but we can still be knowledgeable about them, their relevance to our practice, and thus our location in the broader landscape. When considering an entire landscape, claims to knowledgeability are an important aspect of learning as a social process.[5]

Learning as a journey through a landscape: identification and dis-identification

If a body of knowledge is a landscape of practice, then our personal experience of learning can be thought of as a journey through this landscape. Reflecting on our own trajectories as learners, most of us will be amazed at how many practices we have engaged in, dabbled in, visited, encountered, or avoided over the years. In some cases, joining or leaving a practice involved crossing a significant boundary and constituted a major event or transition.

As a trajectory through a social landscape, learning is not merely the acquisition of knowledge. It is the becoming of a person who inhabits the landscape with an identity whose dynamic construction reflects our trajectory through that landscape. This journey within and across practices shapes who we are. Over time it accumulates memories, competencies, key formative events, stories, and relationships to people and places. It also provides material for directions, aspirations, and projected images of ourselves that guide the shaping of our tra-jectory going forward. In other words, the journey incorporates the past and the future into our experience of identity in the present.

Participation in a landscape provides the constitutive texture of an experience of identity. Through our journey, the landscape shapes our experience of ourselves: practices, people, places, regimes of competence, communities, and boundaries become part of who we are. Shaped by our journey through the landscape, our identities come to embody the landscape through our experience of it. They become personalized reflections of the landscape, its practices, and its boundaries. As a workbench for our learning, our identities replay and rework these relationships. Using our own experience as an example, we are both theorists and consultants. This boundary between practices is something we constantly carry in ourselves. And we have to manage it. When do we bring out what part of ourselves? Does our theorist side feel betrayed if we use a simpler but less accurate term to describe a phenomenon to a client? Does our consultant side feel threatened when we feel energized by an idea with little concern for what our client would be able to do with it on Monday? We feel torn at times and wonder whether we can be competent in both. Overall, however, we enjoy the straddling of this boundary and its mirror-image inside. We find it productive, even while it is challenging identity work where boundaries that exist in the landscape reflect and replay in our identities.

Not all the practices we interact with or the boundaries we cross have the same significance, of course. Our journey creates a variety of relationships to locations in the landscape. Some we enter fully and some we visit, merely catch a glimpse of, or ignore altogether. Some we explore deeply and some remain foreign. With some we identify strongly, with others lightly, and with many not at all. Some we exit and some we distance ourselves from. The danger of the journey metaphor might be to suggest that these relationships are merely individual decisions. The landscape, however, is well colonized and some hills are well guarded. Some communities may welcome us, while others may reject us. The experience can be one of painful marginalization or merely the chance to move on. Through it all, the journey shapes us via experiences of both identification and dis-identification.

Finding oneself in a landscape: modes of identification

We can only participate actively in a few practices in a landscape. Even so, many practices we don't personally participate in can become part of our experience and contribute to our identities. To describe how we inhabit a landscape of practice and build our identities in it, it is useful to distinguish between three distinct modes of identification[6] that position our learning in that landscape.

Engagement: this is the most immediate relation to a landscape of practice – engaging in practice, doing things, working on issues, talking, using and producing artifacts, debating, and reflecting together. On our learning journey, engagement gives us direct experience of regimes of competence, whether our engagement is a visit or a lifetime commitment, whether the result is an experience of competence or incompetence, and whether we develop an identity of participation or non-participation. Still there is no substitute for direct engagement in practice as a vehicle for learning the competence of a community.

Imagination: as we journey through a landscape we are also constructing an image of the landscape that helps us understand who we are in it. If you work as a nurse in a given hospital, you know that there are countless other nurses working in other hospitals and you can use your imagination to create a picture of all these nurses and see yourself as one of them. We use such images of the world to locate and orient ourselves, to see ourselves from a different perspective, to reflect on our situation, and to explore new possibilities. The world provides us with many tools of imagination and material for the work of imagination (e.g., language, stories, maps, visits, pictures, TV shows, role models, etc.). These images are essential to our interpretation of our participation in a landscape. Imagination can create relations of identification that are as significant as those derived from engagement.[7]

Alignment: our engagement in practice is rarely effective without some degree of alignment with the context – making sure that activities are coordinated, that laws are followed, or that intentions are implemented. If you work as an architect, it is essential to know how to produce plans that will allow members of various trades to contribute to the construction of a well-designed building. Enabling alignment around your design across the landscape is part of your identity as a professional. Note that the notion of alignment here is not merely compliance or passive acquiescence; it is not a one-way process of submitting to external authority or following a prescription. Rather it is a two-way process of coordinating enterprises, perspectives, interpretations, and contexts so that action has the effects we expect. Following directions or negotiating a plan are forms of alignment as are enlisting a colleague's collaboration or convincing a manager to change a policy. Whichever way they go, these processes of alignment give rise to relations of identification: applying the scientific method, fighting a law we find unjust, abiding by a moral code, joining a strike, or recycling are all processes of alignment that can become very deep aspects of our identities.

These different modes of identification are ways to make sense of both the landscape and our position in it. All three can result in identification or dis-identification, but with different qualities and potentials for locating ourselves in the landscape.

Identification at multiple levels of scale

Relationships of identification and dis-identification created through the various modes can be local but they can also extend across the whole landscape. All three modes function both inside practices and across boundaries:

- Engagement is typical of participation in the communities we belong to, but it can also be a way to explore a boundary if we can have enough access to another community of practice willing to engage with us.

- Imagination functions inside a community as members make assumptions about each other, recall the past, and talk about their future, but it can also travel without limits and is a way to experience identification way beyond our immediate engagement.
- Alignment is a central element of a community's local regime of competence, but it is also essential to the functioning of broader systems, such as agreeing on the strategy of an organization, deciding on the laws of a country, or enlisting stakeholders in addressing a global challenge.

Operating within and across practices, the combination of these different modes produces identification at multiple levels of scale all at once. For instance, teachers can identify (or dis-identify) with the teachers in their department, school, district, region, discipline, country, and even with all teachers in the world. Resonance may be stronger at some levels than others. Some teachers may identify most strongly with their school, some with their discipline, and some with their national curriculum. With some levels they may actively dis-identify, for instance, by dismissing the relevance of a regional policy. But this ability to define our identities at multiple levels of scale is essential to locating ourselves in a landscape that extends beyond the practices we are directly involved in.

Knowledgeability in a nexus of identification

While these modes of identification are distinct, it is in combination that they are the most effective. Engagement without imagination or alignment is at risk of local blindness – this is the way we do things here because we have always done them this way. Alignment without engagement or imagination often leads to unthinking compliance. Neither engagement nor alignment by themselves will necessarily provide material to develop a solid sense of orientation in the landscape. Imagination is needed to reflect, see oneself in a broader context, or envision a different future. But imagination by itself can be floating and therefore gains from being anchored in engagement and translated into alignment. Becoming productive in a landscape depends on one's ability to leverage the complementarity of these processes.

Through a combination of engagement, imagination, and alignment, participation in a landscape creates a complex nexus of identification and dis-identification. Our trajectory develops sequentially as we travel through the landscape and carry our identity across contexts. It is also simultaneous as we experience identification with multiple locations and boundaries at any given time. We experience all these forms of identification at once and in one body – whether they merely coexist, complement, enhance, or conflict with each other.

An interesting question is: how does this nexus of identification become a coherent experience of knowledgeability? We expect practitioners to be competent in their own practice; and we also expect them to be knowledgeable with respect to practices in the landscape relevant to their specialization. When engaged in the provision of a service, practitioners act as representatives of the relevant landscape of practices, some of which they will directly engage in, some of which will have a direct impact on their access to resources for learning, and some of which are much more distant. Practitioners 'represent' this landscape through experiencing:

- Their own forms of competence in key communities of practice
- Their participation in multi-disciplinary work, where working itself is a direct boundary encounter with other disciplines
- Their relationships of engagement, imagination, and alignment with regard to various practices in the landscape
- Their struggle with the boundaries among practices, which can take place through all three modes of identification, but is not less significant for being vicarious, whether it involves imagination or an attempt at alignment.

Knowledgeability entails translating this complex experience of the landscape, both its practices and their boundaries, into a meaningful moment of service. The ability to do this depends on the depth of one's competence in one or more core practice(s), which ground the experience of the landscape in specific locations; and it also depends on one's knowledgeability about other practices and significant boundaries in the landscape. In this sense, knowledgeability is not defined with respect to the regime of competence of any single community, but within a broader landscape that includes a set of practices beyond a person's ability to claim competence in all. We will use the term *knowledgeability* to refer to the complex relationships people establish with respect to a landscape of practice, which make them recognizable as reliable sources of information or legitimate providers of services. Like competence, knowledgeability is not merely an individual characteristic. It depends on claims to have insights into practices in the landscape and social expectations concerning the value of these practices. Whereas claims to competence are negotiated within the politics of competence of a community of practice, claims to knowledgeability are negotiated within the politics of knowledge in a landscape of practice.

Learning to become a practitioner is not best understood as approximating better and better a reified body of knowledge. Rather it is developing a meaningful identity of both competence and knowledgeability in a dynamic and varied landscape of relevant practices.

Knowledgeability as the modulation of identification

Knowledgeability is a complex achievement. It combines many relationships of identification and dis-identification through multiple modes. These relationships to the landscape are resources and fragments of experience to be assembled dynamically in moments of engagement in practice. Practitioners need to negotiate their role, optimize their contribution, know where relevant sources of knowledge are, and be practiced at bringing various sources of knowledge to bear on unforeseen and ambiguous situations. From this perspective, knowledgeability is an improvisational dance in which identification is modulated: in a given context, which sources of accountability to identify with and to what extent are these expressible?[8]

Identification and accountability

Identification is a key factor in shaping knowledgeability because it implies accountability. Over the course of our journey, we encounter countless practices where we have no competence, and never will, by choice or necessity. How we experience such non-participation depends very much on our form of identification with a practice. We said earlier that we were happy not to be lawyers after seeing the series of thick volumes on our friend's shelf. We are not embarrassed to say that their content is largely incomprehensible to us; this has not led us to have an identity crisis. Our identities are not invested in that practice and therefore we don't feel accountable to this collection of big books or other sources of knowledge that our friend would find essential.

By contrast if we are caught misquoting, misunderstanding, or not having read a major piece of work in social learning theory (which happens more often than we like to admit), it does pose a challenge to our identities. We hold ourselves accountable to this regime of competence because our identities are invested in this community. Similarly, but to a lesser degree, we feel accountable to a broader set of academic communities as we need to be knowledgeable about work in neighboring communities, in social theory, for instance.

When one considers a whole landscape, accountability gets more complicated. Should a nurse be accountable to a university curriculum, to research, to management, to regulations? To all of them? What about close colleagues? What about personal experience? This often depends on the context. In any given situation, which sources of accountability matter? Does the new regulation apply to this specific case? What did 'they' intend with it anyway? Do I follow the advice of a colleague? She seems competent and she hangs out with reliable people. Should a recent directive from management trump all other considerations? They could not possibly mean that. Can I trust my own experience? Is it up to par? What about this paper about recent research that seems to cast some doubt on prevailing wisdom? The statistical analysis seemed a bit shoddy. If a practitioner serving a client represents the whole landscape of practice for that person, then in each moment of service, he or she has to resolve the question of where to be accountable. This dynamic modulation of accountability is quite a dance of the self, especially where there are conflicts at boundaries in the landscape.

Identification and expressibility

We have mentioned earlier that our accountability across the boundary between academe and consulting complicates our lives. It provides interesting resources for knowledgeability, but the knowledgeability that we derive from walking that boundary is not expressible in all contexts. Often our identification with being both theorists and practitioners is not fully expressible either in a consulting assignment or in an academic discussion.

Certain aspects of one's identity will be more or less expressible in a situation – a competence gained through engagement in a shady practice, an imagined future such as the dream of becoming a novelist, or identification with a moral standard that demands alignment, like being a vegetarian. In your team, how expressible is your passion for origami, your gender, your religion, or your experience as a parent? And how personally important or practically useful is it that each of these be expressible? In a given context, how much of one's full range of experience is expressible? And when does it matter? What level of identification is associated with inexpressible regions of knowledgeability, with what consequences for one's experience of participation?

To be fully realized, knowledgeability in a landscape requires that accountability to one location be expressible in another. But accountability and expressibility can be in conflict. Many students with substantial practical experience decide not to express this experience when they go to the university to gain a qualification. There, they become expert students accountable to the genre of academic writing. They feel that they have to ignore their experience of practice to fit the academic model when composing a term paper. Conversely, when they are at work, many find it difficult to make use of theory to rethink a vexing problem. Crossing a boundary can force one to marginalize aspects of identity if some forms of identification from one context conflict with claims to competence in another context. Such marginalized aspects of identity can even become completely inexpressible.

Modulating identification

One way to conceptualize learning in landscapes of practice is to think of knowledgeability as the modulation of identification. This takes place across multiple potential sources of accountability and contexts of expressibility. It is sometimes a matter of personal choice and sometimes a reflection of the landscape – often a bit of both. As the world becomes more complex, there are an increasing number of locations in the landscape that can act as sources of identification or a context for expressibility. Should I keep track of that blog, read that scientific journal, follow that Twitter stream, subscribe to that website, go to that conference, or join that online discussion board? How do I modulate my identification with various locations in an increasingly complex landscape? How does the modulation of identification and dis-identification create an individualized claim to

Figure 1.1 A landscape ...
Public domain picture courtesy of U.S. Library of Congress (http://www.loc.
gov/pictures/item/2001703477/)

knowledgeability over time and across contexts? Are there places in which my identification across the board is expressible? Negotiating a manageable identity of knowledgeability is becoming quite a task. It is a central challenge for professional learning today – and to a large extent, for learning more generally.

Moving on

Theory is a lens through which to see the world. We invite you to put on this lens for a moment to reflect on your own trajectory through a landscape. Behind you. Ahead. What are the locations you identify with? What are those you don't? How accountable do you feel to their practice, their competence, their perspective?

What does your journey through the landscape look like? Have you been to the top of a hill, a master practitioner, your identity secure in the regime of competence of that practice? What were the boundaries that distinguished your hill from neighboring ones? What challenges did that evoke?

Or have you covered lots of ground, walking in the valleys, trekking up different hills only to resume your path? Does your journey look like a series of expeditions, an odyssey, a constant flight, or a search for home? Have you crossed a boundary that has challenged your sense of who you are?

Are there places where your accountability to one community, your engagement in its practices, is inexpressible in another? Do you feel that you can be fully yourself there? Do you modulate your identification to establish a distance between you and their practices? Do you feel less accountable? Or do you embrace the tension between the perspectives, reworking the boundary in your own experience? How does this add to your knowledgeability of the landscape?

This is a snapshot of you on your journey, with your history and your aspirations, the result of points of inflection along the way, a mix of intentionality and circumstance, triumphs and failure, rejection and acceptance. It is your identity.

Perhaps one day we will visit your landscape and you will be able to tell us where to visit, what to look out for, and who we'll cross paths with. And we'll thank you for your knowledgeability. And for the opportunity to expand ours. Then, together or separately, we'll move on.

Notes

1. The emerging area of practice-based theorizing on knowledge and learning in organizations has produced a rich literature in the last two decades. Authors have focused on various aspects of practice, for example the life of documents in practice (Brown and Duguid, 1996), the relation between canonical knowledge and knowing in practice (Cook and Brown, 1999), managing knowledge across boundaries (Carlile, 2004), knowing through the senses (Strati, 2007), the embeddedness of technology in practice (Orlikowski, 2007), and the nexus between practice, learning, and change (Hager, Lee, and Reich, 2012). Gherardi (2006) has focused on knowledge across a multiplicity of practices in organizations and provides a useful summary of the field of practice-based studies (2009). The focus on practice extends beyond organizational studies, as argued by Shatzki, Korr-Cetina, and Savigny in their book *The Practice Turn in Contemporary Theory* (2001).
2. This is related to Silvia Gherardi's notion of the 'texture' of organizational knowledge and the conception of organization as a texture of interrelated practices in her book *Organizational Knowledge: The Texture of Workplace Learning* (2006). The notion of landscape, however, emphasizes the perspective of a contested terrain colonized by various communities that claim the right to define competence in their domain.
3. The notion of landscape of practice also differs from that of a 'network of practice' which Brown and Duguid (2001) propose to distinguish close-knit communities from looser networks oriented to the same practice. We are less concerned with the different types of social formations that can sustain a given practice than we are with the multiplicity of practices involved, the importance of boundaries among them, and with problematizing identification and knowledgeability across these boundaries.
4. Because this misleading simplification makes things easier pedagogically for all stakeholders in educational settings, Spiro and colleagues (1987) call it appropriately a 'conspiracy of convenience.'
5. The term knowledgeability was already present in early versions of the theory (see Lave and Wenger, 1991, and Lave, 2008) to insist that the outcome of participation in practice is always an embodied state of the living person rather than just knowledge. Giddens (1984) also uses the term to refer to the state in which members of society act with some general knowledge about their society and its norms (though he is

careful to insist that acting knowledgeably does not exclude unintended consequences, and therefore that knowledgeability is always partial). We use the term in alignment with these two senses, but now more specifically in contrast to competence to define two types of relationships to a landscape of practice.

6. These modes were called 'modes of belonging' in Wenger (1998), but we now think that the term 'mode of identification' is more accurate.

7. We use imagination here in the sense proposed by Benedict Anderson (1983) to describe nations as 'imagined communities': it does not connote fantasy as opposed to factuality. Knowing that the earth is round and in orbit around the sun, for instance, is not a fantasy. Yet it does require a serious act of imagination. It requires constructing an image of the universe in which it makes sense to think of our standing on the ground as being these little stick figures on a ball flying through the skies. This is not necessarily an image that is easy to derive from just engaging in activity on the earth. Similarly, thinking of ourselves as members of a community such as a nation requires an act of imagination but it is no less 'real' for involving imagination. Benedict Anderson notes that people are ready to kill and die for their 'imagined' nations.

8. See Wenger (2009) for an initial discussion of issues of accountability and expressibility.

References

Anderson, B. (1983) *Imaginary Communities*. London: Verso.

Brown, J. S. and Duguid, P. (1996) The social life of documents (Introduction by Esther Dyson). *First Monday*, 1, 1, May issue. Available at http://firstmonday.org/ojs/index.php/fm/article/view/466/387 (accessed February 18, 2014).

Brown, J. S. and Duguid, P. (2001) *The Social Life of Information*. Cambridge, MA: Harvard Business School Press.

Carlile, P. (2004). *Transferring, Translating and Transforming: An Integrative Framework for Managing Knowledge across Boundaries*. Providence, RI: Organization Science.

Cook, S. and Brown, J. S. (1999) Bridging epistemologies: the generative dance between organizational knowledge and organizational knowing. *Organizational Science*, 10, 4: 381–400.

Foucault, M. (1970) *The Order of Things*. New York: Pantheon.

Gherardi, S. (2006) *Organizational Knowledge: The Texture of Workplace Learning*. Oxford, UK: Wiley-Blackwell.

Gherardi, S. (2009) Knowing and learning in practice-based studies: an introduction. *The Learning Organization*. Special issue, 16, 5: 352–359.

Giddens, A. (1984) *The Constitution of Society: Outline of the Theory of Structuration*. Berkeley, CA: California University Press.

Hager, P., Lee, A., and Reich, A. (eds) (2012) *Practice-Theory Perspectives on Professional Learning*. Dordrecht: Springer Verlag.

Lave, J. (2008) Epilogue: situated learning and changing practice. In A. Amin and J. Roberts (eds), *Community, Economic Creativity, and Organization*. Oxford, UK: Oxford University Press.

Lave, J. and Wenger, E. (1991) *Situated Learning: Legitimate Peripheral Participation*. New York: Cambridge University Press.

Orlikowski, W. J. (2007) Sociomaterial practices: exploring technology at work. *Organization Studies*, 28, 9: 1435–1448.

Schatzki, T. R., Knorr-Cetina, K. D., and Von Savigny, E. (eds) (2001) *The Practice Turn in Contemporary Theory*. London: Routledge.

Spiro, R. J., Visipoel, W. P., Schmitz, J. P., and Samarapungavan, J. (1987) Knowledge acquisition for application: cognitive flexibility and transfer in complex content domains. In B. K. Britton & S. K. Glynn (eds), *Executive Control Processes in Reading*. Hillsdale, NJ: Lawrence Erlbaum, pp. 177–199.

Strati, A. (2007) Sensible knowledge and practice-based learning. *Management Learning*, 38, 1: 61–77.

Wenger, E. (1998) *Communities of Practice. Learning, Meaning and Identity*. Cambridge: Cambridge University Press.

Wenger, E. (2009) *Essays on Social Learning Capability*. Available at http://wenger-trayner.com/map-of-resources (accessed February 18, 2014).

Part II

Stories from the landscape

In section 2 we return to a series of stories from different landscapes of practice. The chapters in this section each explore a key theme in relation to learning in landscapes of practice through the medium of stories of practice.

Chapter 2

Failure and resilience at boundaries

The emotional process of identity work

Mark Fenton-O'Creevy, Yannis Dimitriadis and Gill Scobie

In the last chapter, Etienne and Bev described practitioner learning as happening within complex landscapes of practice pointing to the important role played by boundaries between different elements in this landscape. In this chapter we pay close attention to the identity and emotion work which is entailed in personal learning trajectories. Identity is not just an individual attribute, but is negotiated anew in each community we participate in. As practitioners cross boundaries, move between different regimes of competence, and enact their multimembership in different communities their identities are modulated in each new context. We are not, though, tabula rasa. We have social learning histories and we carry them with us into each new situation. As Wenger notes 'An identity is a trajectory in time that incorporates both past and future into the meaning of the present' (1998: 169).

Thus developing identity in a new community involves the difficult process of negotiating the extent to which aspects of identity formed elsewhere are expressible within the new context. Can previous competencies be translated productively into a different setting with a different regime of competence? Does the meaning I make of my practice translate into this setting? Can I make sense of what is going on around me? Do my habitual ways of relating to other people work here? Such transitions also involve choices about the stance taken in relation to identity development. Do I see myself as a novice adopting fairly uncritically the images of myself offered in this new setting? Do I adopt a resistant stance, rejecting others' judgements about competence or appropriate behaviour? Do I see myself as on a journey to the heart of the community or as a visitor, a sojourner whose identity is primarily anchored elsewhere?

This work of reconciling different aspects of our identities is not just a feature of transitions; it is a consequence of multimembership. Take, for example, this trader working in an investment bank talking about the struggle to reconcile his identity in his professional role with that in his home town.

> From where I came from, I grew up in a small town in Florida and none of this stuff really exists like stocks and bonds and things like that. No-one I ever knew growing up did this sort of thing and to me it all seems like a

fantasy world sometimes and it's very abstract. You know, I explain to my mother what I do and I can't, you can't put it into words, it just doesn't make any sense. I am so removed from the daily life of the average person that I think at some point this has got to come to an end. Whether I really believe that or not I don't know but in my head I kind of think this is all fantasy land and one day I'm going to wake up and I'm going to say I had the most amazing dream.

(Fenton-O'Creevy et al., 2005: 1)

In the next section we use three stories to explore the experience of negotiating identity in a new setting. The stories all have a common feature. The protagonists experienced themselves as failing and shared the common experience of moving from a situation where they felt, and were seen as, highly competent to experiencing incompetence.

Boundaries, incompetence and failure

We start with a story about a career transition which entailed movement between identities as therapist, student, researcher and teacher.

Mark's story

At the start of my career in higher education I had a particular experience of failure as a teacher. I got very bad feedback on some of the lectures I gave. Over the years I've looked back on it from my position now where I tend to get pretty good feedback and thought about it quite a lot.

Before I came into higher education I had been working in a therapeutic community in a leadership position and as a therapist. I then decided to move into the business and management world and I became an MBA student. I then moved on from being a student to being a management researcher in a top business school but also at the same time a PhD student. I began developing a particular outlook on the world, as a researcher.

At quite short notice I was asked to take over a course on interpersonal leadership skills for MBA students. There were many reasons why I should have been able to be quite an effective teacher in that situation, as I'd had a lot of time to think about the way in which relationships work and about the ways in which people affect each other, in my therapeutic work with problem adolescents. So I was bringing a lot of relevant skills and ideas from this role as a therapist. I had also been quite successful working in a different role in the interpersonal skills programme; facilitating small groups in experiential learning.

My research also gave me access to key ideas and evidence about the ways in which people interact effectively. And yet when I got into this situation and started giving lectures I failed miserably. We had a feedback scale from 1, very poor through to 5, excellent. After my first lecture I was getting all 1's and 2's. In the anonymous written feedback one of the students wrote 'Who is this clown?' I felt hurt, ashamed, and angry; I found myself questioning whether I could ever succeed as a teacher in higher education. So what was going on? First of all, I think I was quite nervous; it was a new situation to me. I really didn't have any of the craft skills needed for giving lectures. I had 130 people in front of me. I had been put into a way of interacting with people, that I'd never experienced before and was very anxious about it. I'd done a lot of preparation, but the preparation had been reviewing lots of research papers about the things I wanted to talk about. I'd got loads of references on my very many overhead transparencies and I gave them death by slide show.

Of course what I hadn't really done was find a way of taking what I knew from the therapeutic context, and making it productive here. I was throwing research results and theoretical ideas at my audience, but I was failing to connect with their everyday experience of interacting with people. I hadn't found a way of taking ideas from research and making them productive in my teaching and some of that was about me and where I was in my stage of thinking in all of this. However, some of this was the context; I hadn't had the right kind of support in developing those craft skills about delivering lectures effectively. I hadn't had the opportunity to craft the curriculum myself. I was being parachuted into an existing curriculum that I didn't necessarily believe in strongly and had to adopt an existing approach to teaching; 130 people in front of you, in a lecture theatre, that was a given. Some of the problem was that my most relevant skills were rooted in an experience of working with individuals and small groups in quite an intensive way. Where I did work with students in small groups for example in running role play sessions I did well, but I found it very hard to translate this into effective ways of working with the larger group.

I was in quite a hard place, my marriage had recently broken up, I had left behind a work setting where I felt competent and valued and here I was facing evidence that I was not much good at my new career. The area where I was getting good feedback and having some success was as a researcher. Looking back I think this made the problem worse. My identity as a researcher became somewhere to retreat to and exacerbated my tendency to throw research findings at my students rather than really engage with their experiences of work and life.

What happened next? First, I began to develop these craft skills as a lecturer and developed them quite strongly. I was helped in this by forming good mentoring relationships with a couple of senior colleagues who were very supportive and kept telling me I could be good at teaching; a process which made it easier to start seeing myself as a teacher. So I got to the point where I could give lectures and get very good feedback. But that still missed the point because I still wasn't taking the ideas I was engaging in through my research, and the ideas from my former experience as a therapist and being able to make them productive. I think some of it was to do with the nature of the subject matter. Negotiating skills or how to influence someone; this is all about practice. I hadn't really found sufficiently productive ways of engaging with people around those very, very practical skills, at the same time as drawing on all of these ideas and knowledge from other domains.

However, out of this failure one of the things that happened is I did start to think very hard about what it took to produce good learning in these contexts. An important step here was that I didn't have much opportunity to think about how to teach in new ways until I could show that I could do the lecture theatre thing well. Once I developed those craft skills I found it easier to get permission to try and do things in completely different kinds of ways.

> So more recently in my career I've been working on very different approaches to teaching. I think I've probably become quite good at giving lectures. I don't really think I really believe in it though. It is easier to talk about all of this from where I stand now. I've been leading a centre for excellence in teaching and learning; I am a National Teaching Fellow and a Senior Fellow of the UK Higher Education Academy. However, a lot of this has roots in earlier failure; one of the more productive learning points in my career has been this quite significant failure and the ways I had to struggle with who I was as a teacher.

Notice how Mark's narrative has a strong emotional element. He talks about hurt, shame and anger. These feelings seem particularly rooted in the disconfirmation he experienced of his identity as a competent person as his personal trajectory took him across a major boundary between communities of practice. He started questioning his suitability to be a teacher in higher education and retreated for a while into an alternative identity (that of researcher). While he went on to build an identity as a successful and innovative teacher in higher education, he needed to show he could successfully adopt practices seen by the community as legitimate (giving good lectures) before it was possible to innovate and contribute to changes in community practices. In the next story Gill describes similar threats to identity across a boundary of practice and again stresses the highly emotional nature of the experience.

Gill's story

I had a strong record of success as a secondary school teacher. I had strong subject knowledge and a wide range of experience and success. I'm talking about 30 years teaching in several schools in different contexts, a lot of inner city settings, and I felt very strong and very comfortable in my experience. I was highly regarded, seen as very capable and ready for new challenges.

Then I moved to a new school. I still had the subject knowledge but for some reason my teaching was less successful than it had ever been before. I felt that there was something wrong with what I was doing. This went on for several years and my teaching became no better. In fact I think in the eyes of many of my colleagues I probably wasn't very good at it at all. It was a deeply unpleasant and upsetting experience which hurt my confidence. My feelings ranged from anger at being put in a difficult situation to guilt at failing to perform at my best and questioning my own competence. I became quite depressed.

So I decided to leave that school. It's only now where I'm no longer in that setting and once again experiencing a lot of success, when I've come back to a real sense of competence in a strong and supported position, that I have the strength to be able to re-evaluate what was happening before.

Now I can see that my lack of success wasn't only me but it also came from the quality of the context. The school wasn't quite the same as other schools I had been in. The school had a different approach, a different vision of how learning should take place from the one I had managed to develop over many years in many different schools. There was a particular approach to working with pupils which emphasized building long term relationships and pupils being on first name terms with their teachers; rather than a strong rules-based discipline framework. This approach had some chance of success for teachers who saw their pupils every day. However, I taught languages and saw pupils much less frequently. As a new teacher in this school I was at a double disadvantage. I had no existing relationships with pupils and saw each group too infrequently to build up these relationships. I lacked experience of the approach taken in this school. I saw it as a poor fit for the demands of teaching a class that I met infrequently, although I had some sympathy for it. This all combined to make classroom management a very considerable challenge.

The situation might have been remedied, to some extent, if only I'd had good support to develop my own practices in this new environment. However, the school didn't have a very strong management group; they couldn't realize that there was something to do with the school and the situation I had been placed in as well as me that was leading to failure.

I think that because of the perception that it was solely my problem, I got little support and very little guidance. What I now feel is that with better reflection on what was happening at the time and better guidance and a tighter management structure I may have become a better teacher in that setting. Ironically, it was because I was crossing a boundary of practice rather than being a beginner that I couldn't get the support I needed. Had I been a newly qualified teacher, I and the school might have more readily recognized my support needs. With 30 years of experience, it was not so clear to either party and I was left to sink or swim.

I think that, at the time, neither I nor the school realized that I had crossed an important boundary between one practice context and another. In fact between my previous school and this school there was a significant difference in the ways teaching competence was understood. Good classroom management practices were understood very differently between the two settings. Crossing this boundary gave me a problem that I wasn't able to sort out for myself.

In the end it has been quite a profound learning experience, although I would not have recognized this at the time. I do now feel much better equipped to support other teachers' development and to understand the challenges teachers face in moving between different contexts.

Again in Gill's story we encounter strong emotions; anger, guilt and depression. As Turner and Stets (2006: 30) note, disconfirmation of identity often results in powerful negative emotions and multiple strategies are available to us in response. We may change our behaviour to try to get confirming responses from others in the community; seek to convince others to accept our behaviour and the meaning it implies; or withdraw from the situation. We may also change the way we think about the situation. In particular we may de-emphasize the importance of this disconfirmed aspect of identity.

Such disconfirming experiences have important consequences for how we manage engagement, imagination and alignment to bolster a sense of a competent identity. We are faced with choices about whether to disengage and protect ourselves from emotional hurt or reengage and risk further identity disconfirmation.

Do we imagine ourselves members of this community or exercise our imaginations defensively; imagining for example the scorn with which former colleagues would treat practices in the new setting we have joined? Do we align ourselves with the requirements of the new setting or put ourselves at odds with them? The processes by which we negotiate identity as we enter new communities involve both identity-regulation and identity-work (Alvesson & Willmott, 2002). The first refers to the processes by which a community or organization acts on members' identities, whether through formal processes such as induction and training or through informal discourse and participation in the practices of the community. The second refers to the processes by which individuals 'form, repair maintain or revise their perceptions of self' (Alvesson & Willmott, 2002). We see in Gill's story that the identity work involved in crossing this boundary in her landscape of practice involved a negotiation between the school's attempts at identity-regulation (being a teacher involves subscribing to a particular philosophy of education) and Gill's existing identity with different beliefs and values about what it means to be a teacher.

In Gill's case we saw that she was reluctant to align herself with a philosophy of education espoused in the new school. In the face of significant disconfirmation of her identity as a competent teacher, she eventually withdrew, first into depression then by leaving the school.

In Mark's case he had similar difficulties with aligning himself with an approach to teaching which he 'didn't really believe in'. He didn't disengage, however, and managed a kind of provisional alignment with this lecture-based approach to teaching; an alignment which he revisited later in his career, as he came into a position to influence practice himself.

In both cases, it is clear that the processes by which identity is modulated in moving across landscapes of practice generate tensions within individuals and between them and the communities they inhabit. As Handley and colleagues (2006) argue, these tensions may be continually negotiated but never entirely resolved.

We see that the identity work entailed in crossing boundaries between communities of practice is intensely emotional. At the same time, which emotions are legitimately expressible and the form they take are significantly affected by community membership. As Shott (1979) suggests, 'how one interprets one's emotions and, to some extent, *what* one feels, are guided (although not determined) by one's culture and its feeling rules'. For both Mark and Gill their sense of failure and the associated feelings of guilt, shame and anger were difficult to express. This was especially so for Gill whose supposed role as a highly experienced teacher made it even less legitimate to express such emotions.

The next story is one of multimembership. Yannis describes his experience of trying to reconcile multiple facets of his identity and the way in which his interactions with students changed as the weight he placed on different facets of his identity changed. Yannis's story addresses the same theme of failure and emotion at the boundary between parts of the landscape of practice. However, his story is also one of activism in the landscape. He tries to actively bridge between the academic and practice worlds and to support students in navigating this boundary, a theme we return to later in the book.

Yannis's story

'It was surprising . . . I had a feeling of failure . . . One academic year ended and I reviewed the whole process . . .'

After considerable success I was surprised, and hurt, to find myself facing failure in my teaching. The academic results were not that good, and students' questionnaires provided several indicators of elements that did not work. I had a track record of success so why did my students not perceive my academic teaching as successful? I was supposed to be a recognized researcher in innovative teaching and learning methods using technology. What had happened?

Facing this failure in my teaching back in 2005 was painful. However, let's go even further back in the past and dig into the context and the circumstances, aiming to detect and express the reasons for such a failure.

When I finished my ICT engineering studies in the eighties, I was struggling to choose between an academic career and some years involved in the 'real life' of an engineer. Life allowed me to taste both flavors during these first years and I worked with a kind of 'split personality'. On the one hand, I could follow a Master's program in the US and was working towards a doctoral thesis back in my country, Greece. On the other hand, there was a great demand for engineers and it was not difficult to find more opportunities as a professional engineer. Several years of my life passed playing a double role; that of a graduate student seeking an academic career and that of an engineer participating in development projects.

The most striking element from my engineering facet consisted in the way a project was carried out. A client was interviewed in many occasions in order to understand her requirements. Several rounds of internal technical meetings were held in order to 'decipher' the fuzzy words and sentences of the client and potential future users. It was strange! We could not understand them! They did not speak clearly! They did not answer our direct and obvious questions of the type: 'What is the maximum amount of time during which your computer infrastructure can be down?' Endless rounds of negotiations, many answers like 'It depends . . .' or 'More or less . . .', many system prototypes were wasted. Also, a lot of time was spent in analysis of economic performance, or in training issues. I had studied as an engineer, who produces systems and artifacts, computer programs and networks. I was a technical person! Why should I spend so much time in all these non-technical aspects? Probably, I had to dedicate all my time in my disciplinary work related to the construction of mathematical editors and signal processing! Over there, at the academic level, things were much clearer!

A few years passed and I went on wearing both hats at the same time. I worked in a support ICT team for a major ministry – developing applications, training people, and putting things to work. I worked in a small company in charge of designing the software solutions within integrated projects. I moved slowly in my research work, reading, analyzing alternatives, experimenting . . .

Life had many aspects. I was a technical person but had to deal with economic terms, work with many different types of people, understand that a pretty and elegant technical solution failed many times, and assume that there are many different 'truths' depending on the role of each person. My 'academic world' was not reflecting my 'professional world' and it was necessary to bridge them, at least within my personal life trajectory.

Life went on and after several years, my academic 'facet' won! A lecturing position was offered to me in Spain within a new department with lots of opportunities, with lots of room for initiatives and innovation! It was a marvelous opportunity to provide an answer to the 'split personality' situation that had characterized my life. One single facet, that of an academic teacher and researcher, could occupy the major part of my daily life! On the other hand, I could even offer good learning opportunities to my students so that they should not suffer from the 'split-personality' I'd been working with. Thus, I could put into practice some of the lessons learnt from my previous 'professional life'.

We formed a group composed of students and faculty in order to provide support to the technical administration of the departmental computer network. The group was meeting every week discussing solutions, preparing contacts with the users (students and professors), the technology providers, or the university managers. A book came out of this activity after 4 years, jointly written and edited within the group. And everything was taking place outside of the formal curriculum! Finally, a success story! Students were working as professionals within the university and were experiencing 'real professional life'. But at the same time, students could connect their own experience with the formal courses in ICT engineering. Finally, they could experience both facets at the same time in an integrated way. This initiative carried on for more than 5 years, till the establishment of a professional technical support team that left our group without a real task. Such an initiative could not go on forever. Some ex-students of the group joined the professional team. The cycle was over.

However, there was another opportunity that was open for me, as a teacher. I could change the focus of my courses on computer architecture in order to recreate the professional environment. The whole course was redesigned as a long project, in which student teams had to design a product, inspired from current trends. Students played the roles of a processor manufacturer, of a system integrator or a consulting company. And I was playing the roles of the client or the project manager, who was providing fuzzy answers, showing the economic and management aspects of the project, etc. This new intervention, a course designed as a project, was also greatly successful. Students were really involved in the process, academic results were more than satisfactory, and our graduates won important professional positions due to such an experience. Another success story that went on for several years . . .

And such a success story was so influential in my life that I even made a shift in my research facet. More and more time was dedicated now to understanding the learning and teaching process, to develop systems that support this type of learning, to contact pedagogy experts, or even to learn more psychological or social theories and understand specialized educational vocabulary. I was moving in another direction, to another landscape. I was crossing a boundary again in terms of research, in terms of academic career, aiming to reconcile my teaching and research activities. I was aiming to have an integrated teaching and research life. And the whole story could go on like this, successfully continuing my work in the field of technology enhanced learning.

However, one might still remember the first lines of this narrative. It started with a failure story – a course with poor academic results, lots of complaints about excessive workload and even some strong objections to the nature of the computer architecture course as a project-based one. Having a successful and long trajectory of integrated life without 'split-personality' situations is not easy. I entered a period of self-reflection as I tried to systematically study why my teaching performance apparently deteriorated. The most reasonable explanation lies in the new attitude that I adopted when I moved to do research on my own teaching activities. In this case, I was adopting an 'authority' role as a teacher thus freezing my relations with the students, or even that my emphasis was now to show the benefits to the academic community, instead of cultivating the professor-student community. Thus, it was difficult to be equally (professionally and emotionally) involved in the 'teaching' and 'research on teaching' tasks. Although I can be considered rather successful in my research facet, I was getting much less emotionally involved; adopting a much too intellectual attitude in my teaching facet.

The emotional impact of such a failure back in 2005 has already motivated remedial actions and I hope I can move again to a 'success' trajectory.

Yannis's story is an account of negotiating a sense of identity which spans multimembership in different practice communities. We see how his sense of his identity modulates over time as he successively gives different weight to different facets of his identity. As Handley and colleagues have argued 'the site for the development of identity and practices is not solely within a community of practice, but in the spaces between multiple communities' (2006: 650). What is clear from Yannis's story is that this is not only a story of shifting intellectual engagement but of shifting emotional investment. Indeed he locates the reasons for the 'surprising failure' he describes in the withdrawal of emotional investment in his identity as a teacher as he focused increasingly on his identity as a researcher.

So, we have argued so far that negotiating boundaries in landscapes of practice can involve experiences of significant failure and is marked by strong emotions. Reconciling the identity conflicts that arise from these transitions and from multimembership not only generates emotion, but it involves shifts in emotional investment as we experience confirmation and disconfirmation of our 'provisional selves' (Ibarra, 1999).

Identity and emotion at the heart of learning

In this chapter we have explored, through a series of stories, the identity and emotion work that goes on in transitions across boundaries in landscapes of practice and in the experience of multimembership. We have argued that experiences of failure and intense emotions are a commonplace consequence of the identity work that goes on in transitions across boundaries in landscapes of practice. What might it mean to take these seriously as part of a learning process? If learning is not just about 'learning to do' but is also, importantly, about 'learning to be' then those who have a role in supporting learning need to pay explicit attention to supporting identity work. If the currency of such identity work is not just thinking but also feeling, then supporting emotion work should also be at the heart of supporting learning. It is not an accident that we started this chapter with stories about failure. Experiences of failure are an inevitable consequence of moving into contexts with an unfamiliar regime of competence. However, the feelings of shame and anger generated by experiences of failure can result in resistance to investment in identity within the new context. If we seek to enable and enrich cross-boundary learning we should start from the explicit acknowledgement that it involves experiences of failure, challenges to your sense of who you are, even sometimes abandoning cherished beliefs and values. It involves difficult emotions such as shame, grief and anger. Dealing with these challenges is not peripheral to learning. Rather we should explicitly acknowledge them as at the core of professional development and design learning to support their negotiation.

References

Alvesson, M. & Willmott, H. (2002). Identity regulation as organizational control: producing the appropriate individual. *Journal of Management Studies, 39*(5): 619–644.

Fenton-O'Creevy, M., Nicholson, N., Soane, E., & Willman, P. (2005). *Traders: Risks, Decisions and Management in Financial Markets.* Oxford: Oxford University Press.

Handley, K., Sturdy, A., Fincham, R., & Clark, T. (2006). Within and beyond communities of practice: making sense of learning through participation, identity and practice. *Journal of Management Studies, 43*(3): 641–653.

Ibarra, H. (1999). Provisional selves: Experimenting with image and identity in professional adaptation. *Administrative Science Quarterly, 44*(4): 764–791.

Shott, S. (1979). Emotion and social life: a symbolic interactionist analysis. *American Journal of Sociology, 84*: 1317–1335.

Turner, J. H. & Stets, J. E. (2006). Sociological theories of human emotion. *Annual Review of Sociology, 32*: 25–52. doi: 10.1146/annurev.soc.32.061604.123130

Wenger, E. (1998). *Communities of Practice. Learning, Meaning and Identity.* Cambridge: Cambridge University Press.

Chapter 3

Students at the academic–workplace boundary

Tourists and sojourners in practice-based education

Mark Fenton-O'Creevy, Lindsay Brigham,
Sylvia Jones and Ann Smith

As we have explored in previous chapters, crossing boundaries in landscapes of practice is an important occasion of learning. However, a sense of identity as a capable person, knowledgeable about problems and their solution, in one context, may be difficult to express in another. In this chapter we explore the experience of students in practice-based education, as they move between academic and workplace communities, and between different communities in their work lives. We look at the challenges they face in these transitions, how they learn and develop resilience in the face of these challenges, and how they seek to translate learning from one part of the landscape into another.

Trajectories of participation

Students engaged in practice-based learning are engaged in courses which seek to integrate learning in academic and workplace contexts. They face the challenge of negotiating multiple boundaries in the course of their studies. They straddle a boundary between the academic and workplace context, but also typically are engaged in transitions across boundaries in the workplace, both between their current and future work roles and between different areas of practice.

Early writing on situated learning focused primarily on the role of legitimate peripheral participation (Lave & Wenger, 1991). Legitimate peripheral participation describes the ways in which novices in a community of practice learn through participation in its practices as they move on a trajectory toward full participation. As Lea (2005) notes, much writing on communities of practice in the context of education assumes that learners are on a trajectory from apprenticeship to full membership of a community of practice. However, shifting our focus from communities of practice to landscapes of practice highlights other modes of participation. Especially as we consider individual trajectories across landscapes of practice and boundary encounters, it becomes important to consider individual trajectories in communities of practice other than inbound from periphery to centre. In his 1998 book, Wenger introduced the idea of marginal participation, where individuals may be long-term members of a community but excluded from full participation (Wenger, 1998). He also began to consider different trajectories than periphery to centre (Wenger, 1998: ch. 4). Handley and colleagues (Handley et al., 2006) have sought to distinguish between different modes of marginality. Marginality not only arises from exclusion but may also reflect a choice to resist the practices of a community or engage only provisionally with them (Ibarra, 1999). In the context of this chapter we highlight the role of imagined trajectory in relation to participation. Not all participants in communities of practice understand their journeys as leading to full participation; some are just visiting. This is often true for students at university, who are passing through academic communities of practice and understand that their trajectories will carry them outside these communities again. Figure 3.1 introduces a classification of modes of peripherality in these terms. We highlight two crucial distinctions. First, does the participant imagine themselves on a trajectory which lies within the community of practice or on one which is passing through with an endpoint outside it? Second, to what extent do they really engage with the practices of the community; is participation low or high?

In this chapter we focus on students who imagine themselves on trajectories which intersect an academic community but soon pass beyond it. They are visitors, but there are different kinds of visitors. Some have low levels of participation engaging in only superficial ways with local practices; their identities are hardly changed by the experience and the academic world remains a foreign country to them. We have labelled these 'tourists'. Other visitors have a higher level of participation, engaging with the meaning of local practices in ways which have implications for their own identity, while nonetheless recognizing that they are 'passing through' and unlikely to become fully assimilated. We have labelled these 'sojourners'.[1] Of course, some students do see themselves on an inward-bound trajectory to the heart of an academic community, going on to

Imagined Trajectory

		Inside community of practice	Passing through
Participation	**Low**	Marginal	Tourist
	High	Apprentice	Sojourner

Figure 3.1 Forms of peripheral participation

take a PhD and pursue an academic career, but these are a minority and not our focus in this chapter. In line with previous accounts we label the low and high participation positions, those with imagined trajectories inside the academic community, as marginal and apprentice respectively.

The crucial distinction, which we highlight in this chapter, between the inbound member of the community and the sojourner is in their imagined trajectory and the context it bestows for their engagement and alignment with the practices of the community. The sojourner, unlike the tourist, is involved in identity work. This work though is not aimed at assimilation within the community but at accommodation to the practices of that community and its regime of competence in order to function effectively within and beyond the community. Identification with the academic community is partial and provisional. We do not, though, regard this sojourner status as a problem to be overcome. Rather it represents a profound opportunity for learning.

In this chapter we first explore the difficulties faced by practice-based students as they negotiate trajectories across boundaries within their workplace and between workplace and academy. We consider their experience as they enter the academic community; manage transitions in their workplace, including those triggered by their studies; and seek to translate what they have learned in the academic context into something which is productive in their workplace.

We pay particular attention to the development of resilience in this landscape as an important learning outcome for these practice-based students. As we have seen in the previous chapter, a core challenge of identity work is the need to maintain a continuous sense of self in the face of threats to identity across landscapes and over time, and to manage the emotions this evokes. Indeed some have argued that developing this capacity for a continuous and resilient sense of self across situations and over time is a core developmental task (e.g. Lalonde, 2006).

As a vehicle for this exploration we draw on interviews with healthcare support workers studying on a pre-registration nursing programme and their tutors, and on interviews with managers who have completed a part-time MBA. In both cases course participants studied part-time alongside work commitments; part-time work for the nursing students, full-time for most MBA students.

Peripheral participation in an academic community of practice

We turn first to nursing students' initial experiences of negotiating the boundary between workplace and university. These course participants are not just wrestling with multimembership in different communities but are engaged simultaneously in two separate, though interrelated, trajectories. On the one hand, they are engaged in a transition from healthcare support worker to nurse within a workplace setting. On the other hand, they are engaging in an academic community of practice in support of that transition. The first trajectory involves

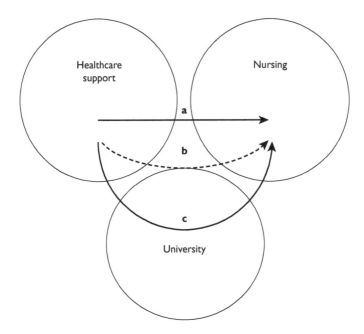

Figure 3.2 Student trajectories

them in legitimate peripheral participation in the nursing community of practice, in their role as student nurse. The imagined course of their trajectory is to full participation as a nurse. On the other hand, participation in an academic community of practice is provisional and temporary. The expected course of the trajectory is not to full participation in an academic community of practice but towards participation in the nursing community and an identity as a qualified nurse.

Figure 3.2 illustrates these trajectories. It can, of course, be adapted to the case of other categories of student.

Line (a) represents the workplace transition from healthcare support worker to nurse. Lines (b) and (c) represent alternative trajectories through a community of academic practice with different levels of participation. In trajectory (b) students follow a *tourist* route – they engage superficially in the academic practices but with no commitment to an academic identity and no engagement with the meaning of these practices. In trajectory (c), which we have labelled *sojourner*, participation is still provisional and temporary but there is a deeper commitment to the meaning of academic practices and to their implications for the practice of nursing. Those on this trajectory are actively engaged in integrating their understanding of academic and workplace practices, and in reconciling their different experiences of themselves in these different domains. Similarly, when we turn later to the accounts of MBA students, it is clear that their trajectories pass through academic communities of practice with a destination which lies outside them. For these students also, we see evidence of stronger and weaker participation.

A parallel might be drawn here with the literature on student approaches to learning (Marton & Säljö, 1976; McCune & Entwistle, 2000; Trigwell & Prosser, 1991) which distinguishes between deep and surface approaches. The deep approach entails what Entwhistle (1997) describes as 'an intention to understand ideas for oneself' as opposed to 'the more modest surface intention – to cope with course requirements'. The former requires an integration of learning with one's existing mental models and has implications for identity work, as identities in different communities of practice are reconciled. The latter avoids disturbance of existing identity constructs by avoiding engagement in the meaning of academic practices. This parallel between trajectory, identity work and deep versus surface approaches to learning is supported by research which reveals greater use of deep approaches to learning among course participants with a stronger sense of their identity as a student (Bliuc et al., 2011a, 2011b).

Entry

Sylvia Jones carried out textual analysis of assignments and interviews with 40 nursing students and 6 of their tutors, focusing particularly on their experience of the transitions between workplace and academic study.[2] The particular focus of her enquiry is the struggle students have with academic literacies. This opens a window for us on their problems with developing multiple identities and in expressing their competence with unfamiliar practices where the regime of competence is very different from that in the work role they occupy and the work roles to which they aspire.

The students are at the beginning of a path that will lead to professional qualifications in nursing and are taking a foundational module in Health and Social Care[3] via distance learning as part of a Pre-registration Nursing Programme. They share the module with students taking other qualifications in the health and social care field. It is important to their story to note that students studying this particular course tend to come onto it with the minimum entrance requirements in terms of numeracy and literacy. They are generally older than students on more traditional courses run by campus-based universities, predominantly women and most have not been involved with formal education for many years. For the vast majority it is their first experience of higher education but they have extensive experience of working in a health context, predominantly as healthcare support workers.

The differences between these two domains, workplace and academy, and the ways in which competence is expressed in each, produce tensions. Many of the concerns expressed by students reflect both the anxieties involved as they become subject to a different regime of competence and their highly provisional commitment to the practices of the academic community.

It's really in depth and sometimes I think, how am I going to remember this or what has this got to do with nursing and that question has come up a lot 'what's that got to do with nursing?' and you've really got to dig deep to try and think well . . . if you understand how that works it might help when you're looking after somebody with that problem, but without that you think well that's – I can't understand why I need to learn that.

The study programme is designed to introduce frameworks and ideas that many of these students did not see as immediately relevant. However, the students did not give this 'book learning' any intrinsic value in itself and only valued it when they saw it directly related to caring for patients and clients. Modules do contain such material but the (academic) course designers also seek to provide a broader perspective and enhance students' capacity for critical reflection. Most students came into study looking for knowledge which provides guidance in particular situations or specific technical skills.

It's the study I find the hardest . . . that question has come up, 'what's that got to do with nursing?' I can't understand why I need to learn that.

At the beginning of their journey, some students could not relate the academic content of the course to their future as a nurse. In their essays, they had to express their competence through describing, comparing and contrasting models of care, rather than enacting these in the workplace. This did not fit with their emerging identities as a nurse, whom they saw as a carer and a doer rather than as an abstract thinker. This discomfort can also be accentuated by the apparent gulf between academic prescription and the reality of life on the ward. As Eraut notes, the 'body of knowledge' for professionals is not simply practical but also ideological.

Some of this theory of the applied field is concerned with the application of theories and concepts from scientific disciplines; some is based on empirical research and conceptual frameworks peculiar to the applied field; some is based on the elaboration of practitioner maxims and practical principles; some is based on what can best be described as a preferred view or ideology of the occupation, a theoretical justification of its purposes and practices in terms of moral principles, views of society and occupational beliefs about the effectiveness of various practices. This last aspect of 'applied field' theory is strongest in occupations based on personal interaction with clients, where there is a strong tendency to construct theories of practice which are ideologically attractive but almost impossible to implement.

(Eraut, 2004: 204–205)

The nursing students were also extremely anxious about writing. For many the loss of confidence as they grappled with unfamiliar modes of expression was a major barrier to expressing their workplace competence.

> I'm always worried about my grammar, and the way that – you know – the style of writing. I'm always confident in what I'm doing, you know the practical side of it. I'm very confident in practical things, but it's putting it down on paper in a style and way, and using the correct grammar which makes you feel a bit vulnerable, I'm not as confident.

Within the 'study skills' approach often adopted in higher education, this kind of difficulty is often framed as a problem with the cognitive skills of writing. However, the academic literacies approach which has become increasingly influential over the last decade focuses on academic literacies as social practices. It views problems with student writing as issues at the level of ways of knowing and identities rather than skill or socialization. In this view the literacy demands of the curriculum involve a range of communicative practices including understanding the different demands of genres, fields and disciplines and the different implicit demands between different courses and settings. As one paper on academic literacies notes:

> From the student point of view, a dominant feature of academic literacy practices is the requirement to switch practices between one setting and another, to deploy a repertoire of linguistic practices appropriate to each setting and to handle the social meanings and identities that each evokes.
>
> (Lea & Street, 1998)

For example, for the students introduced above, the modes of writing demanded of them change not only as they moved between workplace and university but also as they moved between different course modules.

Looking at student writing in an assignment from their introductory module gives some indication of these boundary tensions and the boundary learning that writing the assignments affords. In their writing, students have to learn how to frame knowledge and concepts in ways that are acceptable to the academic disciplinary context. To do this, students need to learn practices governed by the values of their academic subject area, in this case, health and social care. They have to develop the appropriate 'voice' in their writing in order to show their learning and hence competence. They also have to learn what practitioners on the periphery of a community (i.e. students) are allowed to profess and, more tellingly, the style in which they are required to express this knowledge.

The module uses case studies to engage students with models and principles. This mode of presentation attempts to form links between the two domains inhabited by the students. An example of such an assignment is shown here.

> In what ways did the role Anwar Malik played as a hospital patient contrast with the
> expert patient role he had been encouraged to play by the Hilltop diabetes clinic?
> Describe the two roles and explain the differences between them making reference to
> the biomedical model.

The assignment is based on a case study about care of a diabetic patient, Anwar, and it is written as an account of incidents in his life when he receives care from a nurse at his local doctor's practice and from a hospital. This case study is used to teach models of patient care: *passive patient, expert patient, and the hospital model*, and students have to show an understanding of these in their assignment.

The assignments that gain the most marks frame the case studies to develop categories of *passive patients* and *expert patients* and illustrate these categories from incidents in the case study. The extract below shows an assignment that was highly valued by the tutor. The student had framed her assignment around the categories as shown in the opening of the paragraph.

> On entering hospital, Anwar's first role is as a passive patient and is expected to become
> compliant with all the health professional's instructions. The hospital role is the extreme
> version of the sick role (Unit 2, P90). As a hospital patient, Anwar is no longer seeking
> just medical advice as he now needs medical intervention. He is excused his normal
> duties for his own care and the hospital have taken over the responsibilities of Anwar's
> health and care needs. The role change started from the journey in the ambulance,
> which left Anwar feeling very anxious. This passive role was to become more apparent
> when Nurse Kaur advised Anwar that he was no longer needed to self-medicate or
> monitor his diabetes, as this was a hospital rule.

This student structures her reply around roles or models of patient care, not Anwar. She defines passive patient *'and is expected to become compliant'* then goes on to compare the *'hospital role'* with *'the sick role'*. Thus, this student is writing about core concepts presented in the module for conceptualizing nursing care and is able to compare and contrast these explicitly. The student demonstrates that she has mastered the academic framework and can use it to draw distinctions in writing about the care of a patient.

Less successful students structure their accounts around Anwar himself, and make his experiences the framework for their assignments.

> Anwar visited Nurse Richards, the specialist diabetic nurse who is part of the primary
> care team within his surgery. The nurse observed that Anwar was wearing an open-toed
> slipper. Anwar explained that he had bumped his toe at some time weeks before. Nurse
> Richards was concerned that the foot was now gangrenous. He informed Dr. Rees
> Anwar's GP who agreed. The decision was made to send Anwar to hospital in an
> ambulance to see a diabetes specialist.

> Once there Anwar's experience of expert patient changed to passive patient.
> He lay on a trolley in the supine position on a corridor unable to see people around him, although there was no reason for him to be lying down. Sometime later . . .

This student focuses on the events in Anwar's life and the details of the care he receives. The assignment is organized around time, and fails to make the course frameworks the organizing structure. It does, though, give many details about Anwar's care and suggests, indirectly, that the student understands the concepts.

The tutor's assessment of this kind of assignment is that such students '*write somewhat subjectively and anecdotally and get bogged down in detail*'.

Yet, these less successful assignments noted aspects of Anwar's experience that were crucial to his healthcare and showed a tacit understanding of when Anwar was actually behaving as an expert patient and when he was behaving as a passive patient. Noting aspects of patient behaviour and responding to this is an essential element of good care. The students who wrote in this way were not so much having difficulty with making sense of the patient's experience as having difficulty in expressing competence in ways valued in the academic domain and in adapting to a new regime of competence.

Here we see the different levels of engagement with academic practices, which we have labelled sojourner and tourist and associated with deep and surface approaches to learning. In the first example there is a commitment to adopting the academic language and models of the course and using them as tools to understand a nursing situation. In the second the assignment shows some understanding of the patient's situation but fails to engage significantly with the academic frameworks as tools to explore the patient's experience.

These course participants are starting to embrace, to different extents, a new (albeit temporary) identity as 'student' and opening themselves up to a wider definition of their role. As they progress in their programme of study, these students take on a parallel identity as student nurses in their workplaces. As reflected in Figure 3.1, they have to manage and reconcile identities as student, student nurse and healthcare support worker as they work towards an identity as qualified nurse.

Transition

Lindsay Brigham and Ann Smith carried out a qualitative study of students on the same course of study; in this case in the final year of the qualifying route for pre-registration nursing students (Brigham & Smith, 2008). This entailed an initial focus group and in-depth interviews with eleven part-time nursing students. The main focus of enquiry was how the students managed their emotions and developed resilience as they negotiated the many challenges they encountered in their learning journey from healthcare support worker to qualified nurse.

The transition from the healthcare support worker role to qualified nurse status is very significant in terms of work role and professional identity. Healthcare support workers access the programme through sponsorship by their employer rather than individual application, study it on a part-time basis and have a dual role as student and employee. Following their introductory module, students take a placement in a healthcare setting alongside study. They are also required to keep written records of the practical tasks they carry out and compile a portfolio of their reflections on these activities. They have to read and write about theoretical frameworks and concepts that support and enhance their patient-facing practice and write essays which draw on these ideas and practical work. In the workplace they continue to work part-time in their role as healthcare support workers while taking on a role as student nurse in a series of different practice areas.

What came across strongly in the students' accounts, as we explore below, is that they survived and thrived by learning to cope with challenges associated with different boundary crossings encountered in their transitional trajectory from healthcare support worker to qualified nurse: boundaries between different identities within their practice setting; between different areas of practice within the workplace; and the boundary between workplace and academic study discussed in the previous section.

Resilience

Academic work on resilience has its roots in studies of child development where researchers and practitioners noted the marked difference in outcomes between children facing similar risk factors; such as abuse, trauma and divorce. Early work focused on differences in individual traits and to some extent on 'protective' environmental factors. More recent work has emphasized the social embeddedness of resilience viewing it not as an individual trait but a product of the interaction between individuals and their social settings. This work has broadened out to consider the resilience of workers in stressful professional settings such as teaching, nursing and social work. While definitions vary in this field especially in the emphasis placed on individual or social factors, a common definition of resilience is 'the process of, capacity for, or outcome of successful adaptation despite challenging or threatening circumstances' (Masten et al., 1990: 425). Of particular note in recent work on resilience is the increasing emphasis on resilience as the effective regulation of emotion and of identity. For example, Lalonde (2006) in his work on youth suicide in marginalized aboriginal groups has conceptualized resilience as the capacity to manage the core identity work we all face: resolving the paradox of continuity of self through changes in identity across times and places. People change, often dramatically, yet mostly retain a sense of themselves as a continuous person. As Lalonde (2006) notes:

> Though persistence or continuity is foundational to any workable definition of self, we are not born with arguments at the ready concerning how we

ourselves (or anyone else) ought to be understood to change and yet remain the same person.

Lalonde argues both that this ability to forge a sense of continuous identity is learned and that approaches to this identity work vary between cultures. In developing this sense of a stable identity, individuals not only draw on common cultural resources for their sense of self but also draw on those resources to maintain their sense of self through change and over time as they move into new contexts.

Day and colleagues (Day & Kington, 2008; Gu & Day, 2007) carried out a four-year longitudinal study with 300 teachers in 100 schools in England, collecting both qualitative and quantitative data on performance and experience of work. On the basis of this work they conceptualized teachers' resilience as the capacity to effectively manage and balance their identities across three elements of their landscape of practice (our term not theirs): personal (lives outside school); situated (lives in school); and professional (their subscription to professional values and beliefs, and their engagement with external policy agendas). Teachers experienced a stable sense of identity when these elements were stable and in balance. However, this sense of a stable and positive identity could be threatened by crises or events which created tensions between these elements or disturbed the balance (e.g. personal crises, policy changes, school changes or pupil changes).

The boundary encounters and transitions faced by practice-based students provide not just challenges to their sense of identity, but an important location for developing resilience; for building the capacity for successful negotiation of identity change and continuity in landscapes of practice.

Moving between multiple identities

The identity work involved in multimembership is particularly significant for these students as they remain employed as healthcare support workers for the duration of their studies and combine this role with academic study and workplace learning, within their own practice settings and in different areas of practice within their workplaces. Each student is juggling with different identities in working for part of the week as a healthcare support worker and for the remainder of the week as a student nurse in her own workplace setting, at the same time as engaging in course work, in the role as a university student. At the same time in common with many professional roles the work itself can be highly stressful and evoke strong emotions. Interviewees described the challenge of crossing and re-crossing identity boundaries and in particular of asserting a student identity when co-workers continue to relate to them as a healthcare support worker. Often they had to actively manage the expectations of others and redefine the work-based context as a learning situation.

> I went into the multi-disciplinary team, which I am part member of, and said 'I am a student, I'm here in a student role'. So it was important to get the team to recognize me as something other than a support worker.

Individuals interviewed in the study were proactive in identifying workplace learning opportunities and opening up spaces for learning in negotiation with others. They talked about students on other programmes, who didn't have their dual role as students and employees, as being 'spoon fed'. They had to develop a sense of themselves as having a right to be a student and alongside this a responsibility to make the most of opportunities available to get what they needed to succeed.

> It is good to be a member of the [work] team but sometimes you need to step out of that and think well actually I need to learn about this . . . I've got this opportunity – I need to do that now because I will not get that opportunity again.

> I've decided that it's down to me to make things happen so I've just really tagged along with the staff nurse and said 'Can you show me how this is?' and I've learnt a lot from that . . . I've got to get the most out of that and it's down to me.

We made the distinction earlier in this chapter between *tourists* and *sojourners*, those engaging in a surface way with course requirements and those who seek to integrate what they are learning with their other areas of knowledgeability and engage with the meaning of academic practices. Not all students participated equally in academic practices. Some expressed significant ambivalence about or resistance to academic practices.

> I actually went downstairs and said to my husband, 'I don't want to be a doctor, I'm not doing a Masters, look at this'.
> 'Do I really need to know all the areas of the brain, why? I mean I'm not a brain surgeon, it's not going to be something I deal with, I deal with the after effects if you like, how you're going to recover from a stroke.'
> 'It's really in depth and sometimes I think, how am I going to remember this or what has this got to do with nursing and you've really got to dig deep to try and think well it may just happen to – if you understand how that works it might help when you're looking after somebody with that problem, but without that you think well that's – I can't understand why I need to learn that.'

In contrast, others thought more deeply about how to translate 'book learning' into something that had meaning in their workplace.[4]

An auxiliary like myself from the community, we go out and we do our work and we sort of just do things automatically but not really think too deeply about why we were doing that, whereas when we became a student it was a bit like, well you're assessing a wound and then re-evaluation and that, and is it working and you're also looking at other things within the home, looking holistically at 'mmm are they coping? Are they eating right?' all the other things from our reading.

The gentleman had a low sodium. Now low sodium would have an effect on what anti-depressants work, so it was a case of 'oh, I wonder which anti-depressants they were, oh that will be interesting to look up and then go into it'.

Trajectory tensions

Students' identity work throughout the trajectory from healthcare support worker to qualified nurse also involved working with imagined futures. In addition to the ambiguities and tensions around present identities triggered by boundary crossings, students also told stories about fears and uncertainties about the future and what they might become.

As a nursing student I've got the time haven't I. [. . .] As a qualified, that's what's worrying me, I don't want to lose that direct contact with the patients. When I'm doing assessments I like to make sure that I've got time to spend with them, there's no other distractions. You can find out a lot of what people really need if you can build that relationship between you and the patient. If you get close to them to a certain extent, they are willing to tell you things that otherwise they wouldn't.

There were clearly ambiguities expressed here in relation to becoming a qualified practitioner. The story is revealing in terms of the sense of anticipatory loss felt in the trajectory from healthcare support worker to the qualified nurse role. Being a student and healthcare support worker is equated with direct patient contact and building relationships of trust whereas, by implication, being 'a qualified' implies a more remote role. Input is equated explicitly to time but this story and others also reveal a use of self or way of being with patients that involves human interaction, emotional involvement, trust and empathy and the concern that this way of being is less appropriate within a more professional role. This student clearly has worries that taking on a professional identity will mean being more emotionally remote and distant from the patient experience. Here, as in earlier stories we see that not only is identity work intrinsically emotional, but that it also involves learning social rules about emotional engagement and the appropriate expression of emotion. If individuals take on the role of healthcare support worker because of the satisfaction of 'care-giving', then perceptions of a professional role that is more remote and less engaged with patients can create ambivalence and identity conflicts which need to be worked through in the learning process.

Resources for resilience

Research on the development of resilience suggests that resilience develops through supported exposure to challenging situations (Rutter, 2006). For these students too, it appeared to be the challenges, and sometimes difficult and adverse conditions, that made them more resilient and determined to succeed. In particular, it was through negotiating challenges to identity with support from peers and mentors and in using the transitional space afforded by the course that they developed their emerging identities as nurses. An important part of this process was developing the ability to successfully negotiate multimembership.

In facing these challenges these students drew on a range of resources, which we explore below.

Legitimacy of peripheral role and ability to assert 'learner status'

Ward managers sometimes didn't know how to respond to these students on placement, who were clearly experienced in a healthcare support role, and therefore perceived as having more legitimacy to participate. As one student explained '*people expect more of you than a student coming in fresh*'. However, individuals didn't necessarily have the specialized technical skills or localized knowledge of a different area of practice to meet expectations and therefore occupied an ambiguous position in terms of degree of legitimate peripheral participation. In both of the following extracts individuals actively assert their novice status as practitioners in different areas of practice, claiming a legitimate peripheral role that would allow them space to learn.

> And I said 'I've never had anything to do with chest drains'. So she said, 'oh well, what **can** you do?' I'd never even seen them. I'd heard about them but I'd never seen one or dealt with one and it was really scary. And I said 'Well I'm here to learn – what's the point in sending me somewhere where I know it all? That's what I'm here to do.'
> I mean they say go and fetch us something and – is it big, is it little, where's it kept? And you feel a bit stupid, but no I've got past that now . . . I actually just say, well 'I don't know what you're sending me for', I just tell them 'because, I know I appear stupid to you but I've not worked here before and I don't know where anything is, my background is community'. Go to community and I'm sorted, but out here I don't know what I'm doing.

Support of peers and mentors

While the student role was challenging it also provided important resources for managing the transition between the healthcare support worker role and the nursing role. A strong theme across the interviews was of the value of peer support; because they were students as well as healthcare support workers they had a strong peer group and they used this network effectively to support each other both in their academic work and practice and also in their private lives. They actively created transitional peer communities to meet their learning, support and emotional needs. Workplace mentors, tutors, programme tutors and staff on the wards were all identified in different ways in terms of the support they could offer but predominantly course participants relied on each other as a 'first port of call'.

> If we didn't have each other to support each other and talk about your problems and feel that you're not doing it on your own – if we didn't have that I think we'd all feel really, really low. We still have times when we do feel down. Yes, we've sort of got very close over the three and a bit years, we've all had personally difficult circumstances, bereavements and things and we've sort of got very close through sort of sharing how we felt. I think it is one of those courses that in a way you need to feel that you're doing that, you know. It's just so hard.

Griffiths and colleagues have described the 'learning shock' which many students experience on returning to formal learning. Through interviews and a survey of full-time MBA students, they identified the common feelings of '*acute frustration, confusion and anxiety*' experienced by many students as they cross the boundary into an unfamiliar role as a student; a situation in which they have surrendered familiar work roles (Griffiths et al., 2005). They argue that such emotional reactions may be the mark of the most profound types of learning, involving a radical reconstruction of identity, outlook on life and values. While these nursing students had not entirely surrendered familiar work roles, they were engaged in negotiating the difficult boundaries between their healthcare support worker role and student nurse role in different areas of nursing practice, at the same time as taking on the academic student role.

However, whilst in the Griffiths et al. study, the (very heterogeneous) peer groups were often just another source of stress, for nursing students, developing emotional resilience to cope with the 'learning shock' was related to the mutual support they were able to give each other,

> It saves throwing yourself out of the window. You get to a point and you think I can't do this . . . it's a nice feeling to know you're not alone . . . everyone's in the same boat and that's very helpful.

Peer groups were made up of other students from similar work situations and facing similar challenges. They used each other as a resource to 'make sense' of both practice situations and the academic learning that they were bringing into practice. These shared spaces that students created between themselves appeared significant because they were like a no man's land where they could tell their own stories in their own voices to each other without worrying about the rules of talk in more organized professional and academic learning spaces.

> You've almost got to find your own support systems. One of the other girls who lives in York – we are doing the same course, we study together, so say we're really thinking 'oh this ain't going in', you know we'll sort of say 'right' and then try to break it down.

Reflective space

In addition to this external dialogue with peers, the nursing students often talked about individual spaces they created for internal dialogue and learning through activities such as writing in a diary, 'I was so stressed, I kept a diary every day, a daily one', or creating a (non-assessed) learning journal. These strategies helped them to bring the academic and work-based practice domains of practice together in ways that were meaningful to them.

As healthcare support workers working as student nurses in their practice areas they were crossing the boundary into an academic regime of competence where they had to learn new skills. Formal learning materials, in addition to team and mentor support in the workplace, were also identified as important resources in supporting their resilience

> It's probably the mixture of the practice and the theory, about the support I've had from the team, the support I've had from other mentors, learning from them, the literature that I've read through the course, the ability to see other sides as well.

We started the enquiry with a focus on the emotional resilience of individual students. As we examined the student stories it became apparent that emotional resilience was not so much a fixed individual characteristic but part of a process as individuals engaged in challenges in their local context of practice, drew upon the support of others to help them cross boundaries, imagined their future selves and aligned their practice and sense of self to the more global concept of 'being professional'. Resilience was developed in their core practice as healthcare support workers as they drew on their personal experiences in their local contexts and communities of practice but even more so when crossing the boundaries between different areas and domains of practice. The students gained resilience not so much when they were using cognitive skills to acquire a body of knowledge but when they were fully engaged both emotionally and cognitively in making sense, with others, of different forms of knowledge and practice experiences they were exposed to in their complex landscape of practice.

Re-entry: translating academic learning into the workplace

Just as students find difficulties in translating their competence in the work domain into a competent identity in the academic domain, they also find the translation of learning within the academic domain back to the workplace highly problematic. This became particularly apparent in a series of interviews with managers who were engaged in or had recently completed an MBA. For these (part-time) students, their MBA capstone course involved taking an initiative in their own organization which drew on ideas from the course and writing about the learning they took from the experience. For many this was an uncomfortable and challenging experience.

One MBA student described (in an online forum) how he wrestles with the management of multimembership and the difficulties of translating insights between the academic and workplace domains.

> I've struggled at times to see direct links between our [module workgroup] discussions and theory. [...] I've sometimes felt as though there's a tendency to make theory fit the good management discussions that we've been having, almost after the event, rather than theory providing the insight that supports sound management discussion. [... This] mirrors the exact issue I struggle with, in the real world; how to bring [university] theory and my working environment together? I find this a particular challenge, not least because many colleagues will not respond favourably to what they perceive as 'academic management theory'.

Asked about the capstone project, the manager below describes his resistance to the value and applicability of academic frameworks in his workplace context and his gradual grudging acceptance that something could be translated successfully across the boundary.

> Because I did my MBA rather late I got into a practice based attitude 'so what do they know? They're not running companies, these academics.' And I've actually changed my view . . . I still have a healthy disrespect, in other words, 'that's a very interesting theory, give me evidence of where it's worked'. But I suppose I've developed, perhaps this is also throughout the whole of the MBA, a grudging respect for academic theory . . . what I'm saying is I think sometimes I feel like a frigate captain where you say, I've got this great big battle in front of me and I've got cannon-balls flying everywhere, and then somebody says to you 'I want to talk to you about sail design'. 'Not now!' [Shouts.] But having said that, you do need that bit

afterwards; where you actually say, that's interesting, tell me about this sail design. And somebody will say 'well it's x, y, z. And you'll actually be able to sail four points close to the wind.' Ooh, now that's interesting. And that's what I'm saying. In a way I suppose, practitioners like myself need to be pulled away every now and again into the quiet room, and left for a couple of days to sink down. And then say 'let me talk to you about Prahaled and Hamel and their idea of competencies; competencies and capabilities and their idea, "the resource based organization", and whatnot. The importance of the two Japanese guys and implicit and explicit; Taguchi and somebody else' . . . Yes, I have grudging respect for academics and the application of theory; and the ability I think from the course as well to create theory in a way. I suppose in a small way with the process [we have developed] we have created a theoretical process. Yes, a model.

For many of the students the discomfort brought about by the disjunction between academic approaches to conceptualizing business issues and the messy reality they faced in their organizations was quite productive and experienced as leading to new ways of seeing not just their work, or academic theory, but also, for some, a strong sense of this cross-boundary experience changing their personal identity.

When I started [the module] my view of the projects that I was prone to take was very much around business outcomes, demonstrating a managerial impact on the business, making a change for the better, so, it was all around trying to be a better senior manager. What surprised me, the unexpected part, was the personal part; how much I could actually focus on personal development within that business issue I chose, so, I did quite a large section at the end on the personal learning points and that was far more important than I expected . . . I had all sorts of personal learning and stuff going on in my head and I could have written the whole report on the personal learning aspect without the rest of it. That was the big unexpected for me, just how much there was to gain personally out of that course.

Supporting the journey

Courses which are explicitly designed to bridge the academic milieu and the workplace can play an important role in helping students reconcile and differentiate their experience of academic and workplace practices. However, without the right kind of support, such courses may even lead to a greater perceived disjunction between experiences in the two domains. We have argued in this chapter that to understand the experiences of students engaged in practice-based learning it is important to understand the different modes of peripheral engagement they encounter in their trajectories through the academic community and in their transitions in the workplace. In particular their trajectories through the academic community are not primarily concerned with adopting an academic identity. Their engagement with academic practices and identities is highly provisional and largely in service of a trajectory towards an identity outside the academic community.

This transition through the academic milieu provides, on the one hand, challenges to identity and the need to negotiate multimembership and a complex career transition. On the other hand, it also provides important resources for the negotiation of the transition and for the development of resilience. These include:

- The legitimacy of their peripheral role and the ability to assert a learner status
- The support of peers, tutors and mentors
- Reflective spaces.

It could be argued that the principal role of the academic courses is to confer legitimacy on a professional transition. However, this would be to ignore the role of these courses in supporting identity work in the process of work transition and in providing students with frameworks and ways of thinking about work challenges which can be translated productively in the workplace setting.

It is also clear that translation of what is learned in the academic community into productive knowledge in the workplace is a profoundly non-trivial exercise. Students need to learn to engage in this translation process and educators need to support that learning. None of the above should be taken to imply that professionals do not need to draw on a sound base of declarative knowledge and theory. However, it is clear that such formally acquired knowledge needs to be learned in such a way as to ensure it is readily translatable from the academic context into multiple, messy, complex contexts of practice. Drawing on large-scale multimethod research on professional learning with practitioners across 20 professions, Cheetham and Chivers describe the core challenge of professional practice as '*Technically grounded extemporization*' (2005: 140–141). Most significantly, however, our account of students learning across boundaries underlines the importance of an approach to practice-based education that draws the messiness and complexity of practice and the development of student identity into the curriculum and where student experiences of the disjunction between the different communities they inhabit are actively pursued as learning assets.

Notes

1. We borrow here from Siu's work on the sociology of immigrant groups the notion of the sojourner, whom he differentiates from 'the settler' as a foreign national who stays a significant time in another land but does not become assimilated into it. 'In the new country the sojourner has indeed gone through a series of adjustments to his present environment, and he is very likely to be an agent of cultural diffusion between his homeland and the country of his sojourn. The sojourner though can hardly be assimilated' (Siu, 1952: 34–35).

2. Students were taking the Open University Level 1 Health and Social Care (K101) course. This course is a compulsory element in all OU Professional Programmes in Healthcare; it is a required component for healthcare workers who want to train as a nurse and provides both core subject knowledge and support with academic writing. The written assignments of forty students were analysed and interviews were conducted with six tutors teaching the course. A series of separate interviews were also carried out with nursing students towards the end of their studies (see next section).
3. We would like to thank the students and tutors of the Open University course K101 An Introduction to Health and Social Care for their thoughtful comments about teaching and learning on this course and the students for sharing their work.
4. Of course there is no neat dividing line between tourist and sojourner. In practice many students move between the two positions.

References

Bliuc, A. M., Ellis, R. A., Goodyear, P., & Hendres, D. M. (2011a). The role of social identification as university student in learning: relationships between students' social identity, approaches to learning, and academic achievement. *Educational Psychology, 31*(5), 559–574.

Bliuc, A. M., Ellis, R. A., Goodyear, P., & Hendres, D. M. (2011b). Understanding student learning in context: relationships between university students' social identity, approaches to learning, and academic performance. *European Journal of Psychology of Education, 26*(3), 1–17.

Brigham, L. & Smith, A. (2008). *Riding the Waves: An Exploration of How Students Undertaking a Pre-registration Nursing Programme Develop Emotional Resilience.* PBPL CETL project. Open University. Retrieved from http://www.open.ac.uk/cetl-workspace/cetlcontent/documents/4a48d47d36678.pdf (accessed 10 September 2013).

Cheetham, G. & Chivers, G. E. (2005). *Professions, Competence and Informal Learning.* Cheltenham, UK: E. Elgar.

Day, C. & Kington, A. (2008). Identity, well-being and effectiveness: the emotional contexts of teaching. *Pedagogy, Culture & Society, 16*(1), 7–23.

Entwistle, N. (1997). Reconstituting approaches to learning: a response to Webb. *Higher Education, 33*(2), 213–218.

Eraut, M. (2004). Transfer of knowledge between education and workplace settings. In H. Rainbird, A. Fuller, & A. Munro (Eds), *Workplace Learning in Context* (pp. 201–221). London: Routledge.

Griffiths, D., Winstanley, D., & Gabriel, Y. (2005). Learning shock. *Management Learning, 36*(3), 275.

Gu, Q. & Day, C. (2007). Teachers' resilience: a necessary condition for effectiveness. *Teaching and Teacher Education, 23*(8), 1302–1316.

Handley, K., Sturdy, A., Fincham, R., & Clark, T. (2006). Within and beyond communities of practice: making sense of learning through participation, identity and practice. *Journal of Management Studies, 43*(3), 641–653.

Ibarra, H. (1999). Provisional selves: experimenting with image and identity in professional adaptation. *Administrative Science Quarterly, 44*(4), 764–791.

Lalonde, C. E. (2006). Identity formation and cultural resilience in Aboriginal communities. In R. J. Flynn, P. M. Dudding, & J. G. Barber, *Promoting Resilience in Child Welfare* (pp. 52–71). Ottawa: University of Ottawa Press.

Lave, J. & Wenger, E. (1991). *Situated Learning: Legitimate Peripheral Participation.* Cambridge: Cambridge University Press.

Lea, M. R. (2005). Communities of practice in higher education. In *Beyond Communities of Practice: Language, Power and Social Context.* Abingdon: RoutledgeFalmer.

Lea, M. R. & Street, B. V. (1998). Student writing in higher education: an academic literacies approach. *Studies in Higher Education, 23*(2), 157–172.

Marton, F. & Säljö, R. (1976). On qualitative differences in learning. I – Outcomes and process. *British Journal of Educational Psychology, 46*(1), 4–11.

Masten, A. S., Best, K. M., & Garmezy, N. (1990). Resilience and development: contributions from the study of children who overcome adversity. *Development and Psychopathology, 2*(4), 425–444.

McCune, V. & Entwistle, N. (2000). The deep approach to learning: analytic abstraction and idiosyncratic development. *Innovations in Higher Education Conference 30,* University of Helsinki.

Rutter, M. (2006). Implications of resilience concepts for scientific understanding. *Annals of the New York Academy of Sciences, 1094*(1), 1–12.

Siu, P. C. P. (1952). The sojourner. *American Journal of Sociology, 58*(1), 34–44.

Trigwell, K. & Prosser, M. (1991). Improving the quality of student learning: the influence of learning context and student approaches to learning on learning outcomes. *Higher Education, 22*(3), 251–266.

Wenger, E. (1998). *Communities of Practice. Learning, Meaning and Identity.* Cambridge: Cambridge University Press.

Chapter 4

Multimembership and identification

Chris Kubiak, Sheila Cameron,
Gráinne Conole, Mark Fenton-O'Creevy,
Paul Mylrea, Ellie Rees and Alison Shreeve

Often when educators or researchers explain practice or learning, they look to the individual's immediate context for an explanation. A student's learning might be explained in terms of the classroom environment, for example, or a difficult team member considered in relation to group dynamics. This approach is insufficient when explaining knowledgeability in a landscape of practice. Individuals are involved in a range of different communities of practice and may identify to differing extents with each regime of competence. Living within this nexus of multimembership requires that people reconcile these competing demands. This chapter explores the identity work involved in managing multimembership in, and accountability to, different communities of practice.

Managing multimembership

Everyone has their own particular landscape of communities of practice within which they work, raise children, study and socialize. Some people may find that they keep these different communities separate and are comfortable being quite different in each. At other times, identification with the regimes of competence in two or more communities of practice makes conflicting demands which pull quite profoundly on different aspects of our identity. For example, anyone raising a family and holding down a job will feel torn between their identities as a responsible parent and reliable employee. Similarly, in chapter one, Etienne and Bev described feeling torn between their dual identity as theorists and consultants. Managing different parts of their identity does not simply involve knowing when to express different aspects of themselves. It involves their sense of accountability to different regimes of competence which can mean, for example, that their theorist side feels betrayed when as consultants they use a simpler but less accurate term to describe a phenomenon to a client. These different identities need reconciliation (Wenger 1998).

Reconciling the demands of multimembership can require that people modulate their identification – that is, vary the strength or nature of their identification to the different communities of practice in their life. Different combinations of the three modes of identification introduced in chapter one – engagement, imagination and alignment – can be used to explain the nature and complexities of this modulation. For example, the identification of a mathematics student solving problems 'cook book' style without understanding the underlying principles can be characterized as unengaged alignment. By following the rules of the discipline the student is clearly aligned with its activities even though they are not engaging with its deeper meanings (Solomon 2007).

This chapter explores how different modulations of identification reflect the individual's multimembership. Although identity is personal in that it reflects a personal sense of self, it is also social. Indeed, because some communities of practice promote or accommodate particular identities and not others (Unwin et al. 2009; Niez 2010), an individual may find that they do not fit in that place. There may follow a process of personal difficulty, mutual adjustment or exit. However, people do not simply acquiesce to group norms but talk back and challenge practice. This idea of fit between identification and setting will be used to organize the following stories into those concerned with experiences of congruence and those about incongruence. As will be seen, operating with congruence and incongruence often involves particular personal contortions, adjustments and negotiations.

Stories of incongruence

People may experience their positions in particular communities of practice as incongruent. Practices cultivated in one community of practice may be unacceptable or even offensive in another. Although personally and emotionally difficult, incongruence can present opportunities for learning (Jarvis 2006), though this cannot be taken for granted. The first two stories below explore experiences of such incongruence.

Digital identities – positions along the spectrum

The first story illustrates a position of *unaligned engagement*. The researchers Gráinne Conole and Mark Fenton-O'Creevy describe the first face-to-face meeting of a 15-person research team which fell into a dispute about acceptable practice.

Gráinne and Mark's story

Working on an ambitious project crossing multiple research fields had brought together a diverse and interdisciplinary team. In this first meeting we hoped we'd get to know each other, develop a shared understanding of what the project was about and plan the first few months' activities. A lot of time was taken up with exploring how our background expertise could contribute to the project. We weren't a technologically naive group. We all used various online tools though some were more active online than others. Even so, differences in opinion about appropriate online practice became the group's first stumbling block.

Gráinne

I use a range of social media tools. I have a blog and use Twitter and Facebook. I'm in a number of professional networks such as LinkedIn and Academia.edu. I'm comfortable within these environments, but don't see myself as a technological evangelist per se. I've experimented with and adapted the mix I use, personally appropriating them to my preferred way of working and my professional needs. Being part of the broader Web 2.0 community is enormously beneficial both personally and professionally.

I'd met some of the project members before but didn't know any of them very well. As always my laptop was by my side. I feel professionally incomplete without it. I was using it to look at papers and links related to the meeting though I was also multitasking – checking dreaded email and using Twitter. I use Twitter in different ways. It connects me to a broader community of researchers. I'm learning Spanish and I use it to practise. I use it disseminate and discuss research. I have my own 'digital voice' which mixes light-hearted personal reflections and more serious academic statements. I pride myself on being careful about what I say and feel I have a good understanding of what is and isn't appropriate.

I knew that a few other people at the meeting used Twitter occasionally but that it was unlikely that the rest of the group used it. I'd sent some fairly innocuous tweets (see below) about where I was and what I was doing (my followers have said they found it interesting hearing about my work). I was writing these tweets for several reasons – i) to promote the project as something 'worth watching', ii) as personal reflections on the discussion and iii) to invite other team members to engage in some Twitter backchannel chat throughout the meeting. The tweets all seemed to be fairly neutral comments and in all honesty, I didn't think twice about sending them. I didn't foresee that anyone could or would object to them.

07:13:19	Working on Design and Evaluation Framework. Eileen Scanlon and I will be presenting at today's kick off meeting for xDelia.
09:41:05	Just about to start the xDelia kick off meeting in Barcelona. #xDelia
11:41:02	Interesting intro from Craig Lindley on BlekingeInstitute of Technology and their gaming research - fascinating #xDelia
11:52:34	"Ale Smidt now talking re: neuroscience research at #xDelia meeting http://www.erim.eur.nl/portal/page/portal/ERIM"
12:18:20	Clemens van Dinther from FZI Forschungszentrum Informatik talking at #xDelia
12:19:01	@RebeccaF well done you!!! Fantastic news - bet you are feeling pretty good!!!
13:18:21	Retweet @hopkinsdavid Current poll "What is your main area of interest?". Please answer http://bit.ly/lggr2
23:29:52	"Excellent kick off meeting of xDelia project. Very exciting to be working with gaming researchers/neuroscientist etc. Nice meal too! #xDelia"
Tuesday, 10th March	
05:48:11	Up drawing a compendium map to represent some of the research questions we brainstormed for xDelia yesterday #xDelia

05:49:26	lpetrides Wow productive lady!!! Want to answer some of my emails whilst you are at it? :-)
07:10:32	Drafting blog post about xDelia kick off meeting #xDelia need to get some breakfast!
10:24:39	Doing a compendium map of the research questions for #xDelia
11:07:01	Anyone know of a good web based collaborative mindmap/concept mapping tool?
11:09:27	"@mweller ta! Debategraph was the one that I had forgotten the name of thanks!
12:22:47	Thanks for all the tweets re: collaborative web mindmaps!
12:41:34	HEA benchmarking and pathfinder programme report http://tinyurl.com/aj2scb
15:47:01	Been exploring online mindmapping tools. Think I marginally prefer mind42.com over mindmeister - is this my logical chemistry roots showing?
16:37:21	Reflections on #xDelia kick off meeting http://e4innovation.com/?p=304
16:59:56	Trying to decide best mix of collaborative tools to use for #xDelia - as always a nightmare
18:26:39	@jvvw handwriting??? Archaic!!!
19:10:30	Off out to a cocktail bar in Barcelona! :-)
Wednesday, 11th March	
00:05:38	Back from good meal with #xDelia team. We are beginning to have some good arguments about our different perspectives! Yyeh interdisciplinarity!
09:12:10	Retweet joostrobben Great post on instructional design: http://tinyurl.com/d9525g very similar to what we are doing with compendiumid!
09:16:12	@ErikDuval @davidmkennedy funny was asking same question yesterday! I also thought mind42.com looked quite good.

Soon after, Mark made a fairly light hearted comment about my tweets in the meeting. This ignited what became a heated conversation in the group. Firstly, some people didn't know what Twitter was and secondly there was concern that a discussion in a 'private' space was being shared with a broader audience, without either agreement or consultation. I was surprised that such innocuous comments could spark such a reaction. 'Here we go again', I thought, 'someone spouting off about the "evils of technology" when they haven't got a clue what they are talking about.' The dangers of the 'viral spread of txt speech' and the 'insidious transformation of our kids into 'wired zombies' connected to a sinister worldwide gaming cult of World of Warcraft' came to mind. Whilst I listened to what felt like uninformed arguments, given with academic pompousness, I despaired at even knowing where to begin in terms of arguing back.

I tried to explain what I had published, but nonetheless the damage was done. We reached an impasse in terms of my view that I had a right to express my opinion about things, in whatever manner I wanted (within the norms of professionalisms, sensitivity and ethical considerations of course) and this draconian outmoded view of the world in which I had to seek permission to use my own voice as if any discourse around the project should be agreed by some central committee before it could be released.

Not only did this seem like a sledgehammer to crack a nut, but it seemed singularly uninformed and ignorant. A common 'outraged of Newport' reaction to the use of any technologies starts something like 'What is X, I've never heard of X, I don't know what it is. . .' and then some diatribe about personal infringements, or lack of time to engage. This is a deep-seated techno-fear, which translates into an overarching hostility towards the technology and discrediting its use. There is an air of superiority. I guess part of me felt more broadly disheartened because this kind of reaction is one that I come across again and again in my role as professor of e-learning as I try to encourage my colleagues to harness the potential of technology.

Mark

Unlike Gráinne, I'm not a fully paid up, card carrying member of the Educational Technology mafia. I am more of a visitor to this world. I 'get' the technology and use a number of the tools but they are not a core part of my practice. Some of the practices and assumptions in this world seem quite strange to me. But I'd recently been exploring Twitter, passively following a few people such as Gráinne.

My recollection of the debate had quite a different flavour to it. People were voicing a perceived breach of trust. We were in the early stages of figuring out what we were going to do and this wasn't really fit for public exposure. People wanted to try out ideas without fear of being accountable (yet) for the quality of those ideas either in their own community of practice or by the rather bureaucratic funding organization which had already demonstrated a tendency to misinterpret carelessly formulated language. Dissemination and dialogue with other interested parties would come later but doing this now, with unidentified outsiders made people anxious.

It seemed to me that for Gráinne and others from her field, technologies such as Twitter come bundled with a set of social practices in which openness and transparency were core assumptions. Her message was that 'as you take these technologies up you are entering as a participant in my community and you need to adopt our practices'. Does any particular community of practice 'own' these technologies? Were we entering into Gráinne's community or were we starting to struggle with developing different practices more suitable for a different context?

Increasingly practitioners are required to move out of their disciplinary silos to work alongside others in pursuit of goals falling outside of their traditional pursuits (Edwards 2010). By bringing together a broad range of expertise, this research group can tackle questions that would be difficult for each to master individually. The group bridges a number of different networks which lends the project the potential to generate innovative ideas (Burt 2000). However, the tensions created by bringing people together who identify with and feel account-able to different communities of practice are common. The goodwill which brings a group together can often mask significant differences in assumptions, ways of thinking and use of language. The group's potential power can only be realized if it establishes a shared focus and coordinated effort.

These kinds of negotiations can create personally felt conflicts because they go to the heart of what practitioners care about and feel accountable to – in other words, their identity (Edwards 2010). In terms of the three modes of identifica-tion, this group is intensely involved in the meaning-making work reflective of *engagement*. Gráinne too is engaging in some depth – giving a presentation, mapping research questions and weaving this activity into her participation on Twitter. However, the group's identification is much more ambivalent regarding alignment. The project's design is still in flux and the group and Gráinne are in a state of *unaligned engagement*. This is an uncomfortable place to be, evoking anger, confusion, dismissal, stereotyping and demoralization.

Unaligned engagement may occur many times within a group's life and Edwards (2010) describes a range of boundary practices to help groups cohere. These include:

i.   clarifying purposes and being open to alternatives,
ii. articulating personal expertise and values in order to negotiate practices with others,
iii. knowing what matters to other practitioners in order to 'press the right buttons' when working with them,
iv. a willingness to reorient one's approach, and
v.   preparedness to take risks and bend the rules.

Edwards' list suggests that achieving alignment is not about acquiescence to a group norm but collectively figuring out a way forward that reflects the group's diversity. Maintaining this diversity maintains the group's power. This situation creates a need for tight–loose accountability. The group wants a tight control over privacy while allowing the loose accountability to the quality of ideas which provides the freedom to explore and take risks. While participants are finding ways to reconcile their alignment to the research group and their other communities of practice, openness is essential. When the quality of rela-tionships will enable or disable the process of acting together (Church et al. 2003), it is unsurprising that building trust was prioritized.

The challenge here lies in fostering alignment without marginalizing members at odds with it. After all, if members leave the group, its power and capability dissipates. In the next story, Sheila Cameron discusses her experience of a similar conflict between two disparate regimes of competence. She copes with this dis-junction through a state of *unengaged alignment*. Despite this 'playing along', the experience of managing conflicting accountabilities has a huge impact on her view of education.

Crossing boundaries in teaching leadership

Sheila's story

I'd been involved with our MBA for over 20 years, as tutor, author, course chair, regional manager (of other tutors), and, for a while, director of the programme. About six years ago my university 'bought in' a 3 day leadership programme (LP) from a commercial organization. At first the programme was run by the supplier's trainers but after a while we decided to use our staff to run it. Thinking it would use my experience within the business school, and my spare time activities as MBA tutor and life coach, I volunteered to teach the programme.

As a teaching and practice-focused academic I'd never seen myself as more than a fringe member of the academic community. Their central interest was research. Mine was doing everything I could to support managers to develop themselves. It was only when I entered the LP trainer community with its very different practices that I realized the extent to which academic beliefs, values and ways of working were a part of my identity. Realizing this caused me eventually to question many of our teaching practices in the business school. But first I had to learn not to hate the LP. I shall try to explain why I came close to resigning as a trainer on more than one occasion.

I had expected similarity and synergy from the LP which made the discomfort of becoming a trainer totally unexpected. Both MBA tutors and LP trainers seek to develop management and leadership skills. Both make use of, and seek to develop, coaching skills. Yet conflicts emerged from the start of the 'train the trainer' programme. The first phase of this was to attend the programme as a delegate. Because part of my job is training and observing tutors, it was probably inevitable (albeit unhelpful) that from the outset I used the same framework for viewing the event. This distanced me from the experience, reducing the learning gained.

If the trainer had been one of my staff we would have had a full and frank discussion afterwards about his performance. He told interminable personal anecdotes and lengthy stories about other trainers. He allowed delegates to ramble in the introductions. He presented ancient frameworks as the 'last word' in 'management theory', with no scope for discussion of anything more recent. (This was *really* frustrating as I had strong views about much of what he was saying!)

The programme included a 'demonstration' coaching session with a delegate. In keeping with the general emotional tone of the event, it strayed into issues that were so personal and painful that it seemed dangerous to tackle these without counselling skills. It seemed totally wrong to do this before an audience, and inappropriate on a work course where delegates were 'sent' rather than volunteering. After the demo delegates were paired off to discuss their own issues. Many chose personal problems for this exercise.

These reservations almost caused me to withdraw as a trainer before I'd started. But I put it down to trainer inadequacies – he knew nothing about the organization, so had included lots that wasn't really relevant. Perhaps he was just not very knowledgeable about management, or very skilled as a trainer? I was pretty sure I could do better.

So I carried on with the 'train the trainer' programme, but my discomfort grew. Our training included spending 8 days with an experienced trainer, learning 'the script' for each day of the LP, listening to her doing it, and then doing it ourselves. We were given CDs and a transcript of the LP's originator running a programme. We were encouraged to listen to the CDs many times.

We were allowed to devise our personal introduction, and to revise it until it was deemed sufficiently revealing. We were allowed to substitute a few of our own stories if we had suitable ones, but apart from this we had to be near word-perfect on the script including all the trainer stories. At the end we signed a contract to remain faithful to the script thereafter.

I agonized long before signing. On the MBA, tutors often receive fairly detailed notes for tutorials but if they have better ways of achieving the learning outcomes, we encourage them to share these with other tutors and the module team. Here though, 'following a script' and telling other people's stories felt really wrong, regardless of the quality of the script itself. Maybe ideas of 'academic freedom' run deeper than I'd thought. It did not sit comfortably.

A core tenet of the LP was 'authenticity as a leader'. I could see why the programme encouraged honesty and openness in all participants. But it didn't feel 'authentic' for me to tell a series of stories featuring cancer, infidelity, multiple divorce, bereavement, and suicide to encourage openness and raise the 'emotional tone'. Often the stories resonated with the delegates' personal experiences and a box of tissues became an essential part of my kit.

The worst experiences were trainer meetings. No one shared my reservations. Trainers seemed to compete over how 'deep' they got into personal issues during their sessions and in saying how wonderful the programme was. I could see dozens of improvements that could have been made, but it was like voicing a heresy to raise this for discussion! I realized just how valuable it was as a tutor to be part of a critical community where concerns could be shared. We might complain a lot, but always in the interests of continuous improvement.

It took me two years to feel comfortable delivering the programme. I never felt I belonged in the trainers' group though. I did, however, manage to find scope for some flexibility. The evaluations suggested that some delegates were put off by the harrowing stories and I agreed with my assessor that I could tone them down a bit. This seemed to improve the delegates' experience. I became better at 'appreciating' their contributions to discussion, and at linking these to the ongoing development of ideas.

By the time the programme was withdrawn, delegate feedback sheets were showing universally 'excellent' ratings. Many were reporting substantial changes to their behaviour at work or home after only two days of the course. It seemed that two days of this training might sometimes have more impact on management practice than a 12 month MBA course. This was an uncomfortable thought.

By this point, I had also shifted in my thinking. The 'classic' theory served perfectly well to help delegates reflect on their own management experiences. In fact, the stories were far more powerful than the theory. I began to wonder why on the MBA we privileged learning theory in detail over reflecting on managers' personal experiences and practice. I started to tell more stories in tutorials, and encourage students to share theirs.

I also started to think seriously about the emotional dimension of learning. The extended introductions I had scorned at first really helped create an emotional climate where people felt safe to explore their concerns and question their assumptions. When people were 'freed' from these assumptions, others were genuinely glad for them. I started paying far more attention to helping students to value their experience and what they already know as an *aid to* challenging it.

> One of the LP models showed how we can be a prisoner of our own assumptions if we are not aware of these. I was so unhappy that I repressed any knowledge of it only to later find it in my file, heavily and rather rudely annotated! It was not until I ventured into foreign 'territory' that I became aware of just how powerfully my own mental models constrained me and of the extent to which my identity was rooted in my 'home' landscape.
>
> The LP experience made me really unhappy for a long time. But it had a profound impact upon my role as a tutor. It made me feel more of a foreigner with many colleagues in my academic homeland than I had before. My mental models had shifted even further from theirs as a result of the experience. Paradoxically I felt more at home in the LP than previously, but also far more able to articulate my continuing unease and question some prevailing assumptions and practices.

Sheila's alignment with academic practice means that although she delivers the LP and follows the script for the sessions carefully, she is unengaged. Her identification can be characterized as *unengaged alignment*. Not only is she ambivalent about the legitimacy of the training programme, but she is excluded from the vital aspect of participation which generates the meaning making which creates engagement – negotiation (Wenger 1998). She feels unable to make the practice her own and so she follows the script rather than reconstruct the practice in a way that reflects the experience, knowledge and skills that legitimized her presence in the first place.

Sheila's unengaged alignment appears to be a kind of uncommitted hovering over the landscape, an experience Hodges (1998) refers to as a 'lag' in participation where one may be doing the practice but holding back on identification. This non-engagement is not a matter of opaque habits or automatic reactions. Her discomfort is mindfully analyzed and she presents well-argued positions such as 'don't teach out of date theory' or 'avoid lengthy personal anecdotes'.

In terms of making her difficult position liveable, Sheila employs two strategies. The first seems counter intuitive. She resists the LP's practice before falling into strategic compliance (Shain and Gleeson 1999). She does not keep an open mind but delivers the course with deep reservations, performing the script through gritted teeth. Even so, Sheila's marginalized position yields learning value. Her strategic compliance enables her to participate in the programme long enough to see its value.

Through the second strategy, Sheila connects both the LP and her academic practice to an overarching purpose – the importance of developing managers. She reconciles her grave doubts about the LP's methods with her academic sensibility because her work apparently benefits students. This overarching purpose seems to enable her to maintain a sense of personal integrity across communities.

Eventually, Sheila's multimembership changes her view of the educational process. She is won over by an act of imagination. Viewing the programme through the students' eyes she sees that it offers a powerful learning experience. Through this act of imagination she identifies with the LP and is willing to be accountable to it (albeit with reservations) to the extent that she reconsiders her teaching practices on the MBA. In her earlier days, she would have been embarrassed to do so. She is now not simply aligning but fully engaging in both practices.

Stories of congruence

The previous section discussed experiences of conflict, disagreement and marginalization associated with incongruence. The two stories that follow touch on similar themes but are tales of congruence. As in the previous section, strategies to sustain multimembership are teased out.

Paul Mylrea had worked in journalism before moving into Public Relations. As the Director of Communications for Transport for London, he was at the centre of a terrorist attack in 2005 and found that he had to negotiate his way through a torrent of concerns, interests and demands. Despite the potential for dissonance and identificatory ambivalence, Paul maintains a sense of personal coherence and comfort that is missing in the stories of incongruence. In the following story, he offers some practical insight into his strategies for functional and fully engaged multimembership.

Getting the story across

Paul's Story

Over my two decades as a journalist with Reuters, the international news agency, I spent years travelling the world to explain to a global audience events happening in far-away places. In the British press, journalists are told they have to write for 'the man on the Clapham omnibus', a term coined at the start of the twentieth century to describe the essence of public opinion. Yet in an international news agency, the reader of your story could be in a taxi in Buenos Aires, a tuk-tuk in Bangkok or a tram in Budapest. Each has their own cultural references, their frames that shape understanding of the narrative. You learn to find common human frames to help you get the story across.

It is this ability to navigate boundaries of meaning that makes many journalists successful in public relations (PR). I've held several posts – in Oxfam, Transport for London, the Department for International Development and finally as Director of Communications for the BBC.

PR is a role pinned between different interests. I spent a year as the President for the Chartered Institute for Public Relations, a role I took on when I was with the Department for International Development. The Cabinet Office strongly supported my decision to take this role. They saw it as a symbolic gesture representing the credibility of Government's support for good quality public relations. It wasn't an easy position to be in though. How could I play a part in the reform of Government PR when as the President of the Chartered Institute for Public Relations, I opposed job losses in the profession? Similarly, as the BBC's Director of Communications, I had to support the career development of our PR practitioners without bias for the courses offered by the Institute. By drawing on impartial advice and asking others to address these issues I manage the conflicts of interest. There is a border that defines what I should and should not do, but it's a shadowy line and always shifting.

Here's an example of how imprecise boundaries between quite different interests can be. On 7 July 2005 four terrorists detonated home-made bombs on three underground trains and a double-decker bus in London. As the Director of Communications for Transport for London I found I had to mediate between various agencies each with quite different demands. There were internal pressures on staff to deal with the victims and restore the system. There was external pressure to demonstrate resilience and defiance in the face of a terrorist attack. We needed to liaise with a government which was hosting a summit meeting with world leaders at the time of the attacks. We had to make sure that journalists could cover what had happened without them getting in the way of the emergency services. Actually, we *needed* the journalists to report the messages we wanted to get out to the public. All parties wanted to create sense out of a complex and confusing situation. Yet there was also a tension between the need for standard storylines (apportioning blame and identifying what went wrong) and the more complex reality of issues on the ground.

And then there was the need to liaise with the police. Their investigatory concerns were absolutely legitimate, but could conflict with our needs at Transport for London. For example, we had been testing a system which monitors train positions that day and the police wanted this data to inform their interrogations with any of the bombers who might still have been alive. But they didn't want to make this data public, at least not then. In our opinion keeping the data secret would feed conspiracy theories and the travelling public would lose trust in us. We wanted to show that Transport for London had nothing to hide.

In crises like 7/7, the police are the designated authority with the final say in all decisions. This included deciding what to do with the data on the trains' position. We still have a say but decisions are discussed in an operational group made up of government representatives, the police, security, and anti-terrorism services. This sometimes creates robust discussion but there is another dimension to it. There can be a clash of cultures. The police want to assert that they are 'in charge'. Transport for London want to reassure the public that they will get transport moving as soon as possible.

Reading these different cultures is an essential part of communications work. Any PR practitioner will try to speak to these different interests. When it came to the discussions in the operational group, we needed to communicate in a way that these different parties understood. Voice and language needs adapting as you translate between cultures. The PR specialist has to be able to span boundaries, moving at will across the gaps and barriers of culture, language and understanding that separate different spheres. It's a little like speaking a foreign language. You can develop a native understanding but you always remain an outsider. You never lose touch with your own interests.

These kinds of discussions also involve emphasizing similarities. Despite our different interests, we are all members of a community of communicators. We share a way of communicating and share certain principles about how to deal with things.

> We share a belief in the need to understand each other's position. We also share a history which we can evoke in our discussions – 'remember when we did this in the past and this happened' or 'okay, but what about that time when it didn't work?'
>
> In the case of Transport for London's monitoring system, the decision did go my way and the data was made public. Looking back, handling these tensions involved diplomacy and an ability to represent the interests of Transport for London. But we also had to be willing to set these aside in order to achieve a common position. We were, after all, members of the same community of communicators.

Paul identifies with a range of both complementary and potentially conflicting communities of practice. He is engaged in, and aligned with, their practices. His imagination includes a clear sense of his role within an international community of communicators who need political representation. Also, his multimembership establishes his legitimacy. His presidency of the Chartered Institute for Public Relations (CIPR) arises out of his governmental role. Conversely, his role in government is reinforced by his presidency. He speaks convincingly in the 7/7 negotiations because he is engaged with the wider community of communicators.

Paul employs a number of practical strategies to sustain his identification with these different communities. First, he recognizes that these roles do not afford some expressions of his identification. For example, as CIPR president he cannot be seen to favour his employer. Similarly, working as a line manager he cannot express a preference for CIPR staff training. To manage these conflicts of interest he extracts himself from the situation and finds someone to step in for him. This is not disengagement from practice but rather, is a strategy to maintain his multimembership with legitimacy.

The second strategy relates to his ability to speak to a range of different communities of practice. Edwards' (2010) distinction between interactional expertise and contributory expertise helps explain Paul's multilingualism. Those with interactional expertise can speak the language of a particular community even though they are not able to contribute to the practices there. Paul's reference to speaking to the police's interests, for example, does not suggest membership in that community of practice, just skill in multilingualism.

In contrast, contributory expertise is of quite a different order. Contributory expertise is born out of immersion in a community and the ability to contribute to practices there (Edwards 2010). His ability to talk to the wider community of communicators so that they understand they share similar purposes, a shared sense of appropriate conduct and, as powerfully, a common history reflects his contributory expertise. His clear identification with this community is reflected in the way he has a strong sense of alignment with and accountability to their way of doing things. His imagination evokes this group as an actual community of practice and not just a collection of individuals in competition with each other. This is more than an ability to communicate but rests upon his legitimacy as a contributor to this community of communicators.

Multimembership and identity in a landscape of practice: fine art and education

Paul's legitimacy as a contributor to different communities of practice was a strong theme in his story. In the next story, Ellie Rees and Alison Shreeve also consider the legitimacy needed for participation. Ellie Rees is a practitioner of the fine arts. She undertakes residencies, teaches in various institutions and takes other opportunities to earn money needed to pursue her passion for creative art practice. While working for the University of the Arts in London, helping fine art students to understand the realities of being a working artist, she met Alison Shreeve. Alison is the Director of a Centre for Excellence in Teaching and Learning and an educational manager with over twenty years' experience of 'teaching textiles'. In the following story, they explore how they negotiate their way through the different communities of the landscape of practice to find a way to enact their professional roles. As a co-written story they refer to themselves in the third person.

Ellie and Alison's story

Ellie defines herself as '*an artist who works in education*' and in saying so, she's making a statement about her primary position in the artistic community. Although Ellie initially says that she doesn't belong to Alison's higher education community, her family background leaves her feeling comfortable there:

> there's definitely an element to my person that's very much about teaching whether I'm actually doing that professionally or not. I think I'm a . . . I was brought up in a pedagogical environment. Both my parents were teachers; education has been drummed into me as being fundamental.

Earning a living as an artist is a nomadic existence. Ellie is a constant traveller, unable to set root in any community for very long, yet moving in to work amongst them, picking up and developing her knowledge of various practices. As an artist working temporarily in education she feels she only belongs at the periphery of this world though her increasing involvement with organized higher education makes her feel more 'legitimate' and a part of the academic community. A recent interview for a full-time teaching post, although unsuccessful, and external interest in her academic work feel like further invitations to 'belong' to academia, even though this interest partly stems from the fact that she is a practitioner.

Alison has worked in art and design education for many years. She understands its activities, terminology, issues, and politics – everything that makes up the working environment of higher education. Over the previous 12 years, Alison's role has changed from primarily teaching and course management into research and supporting others to teach, with broader management roles. She doesn't belong to Ellie's world and only tinkers around on the edge, though there are things at work that make her feel at home there as well. Her empathy with fine art is derived from spending four years in art college studying alongside other disciplines. She has some historical and contextual

---

knowledge of fine art, but never considered herself to be a practising artist. Alison's limited experience of making and exhibiting work in local exhibitions mirrors Ellie's fine art practice in a much more modest way. These activities are similar but different to Ellie's art work, reinforcing her feelings of dipping into a community of practice and giving her some empathy with the practice.

Changing roles, changing locations

Over her career Alison has been a student, an exhibiting artist, an educator, a manager and a researcher. Each role represents a conscious decision to develop and to take on new challenges. As she takes on new roles her past roles are still part of her – a 'textile person', though no longer doing any embroidery, a teacher, though seldom teaching. These are indelible parts of Alison's history of participation and remain a part of her identity. These different connections to various communities of practice enable her to still envisage belonging to them, even if no longer practising within the community. There are different degrees of being a part of a community of practice and feeling as if you belong.

As an artist, Ellie's life involves varying degrees of participation in different communities of practice. She has started working with an opera company, but feels like an outsider, not really accepted into the musicians' community. Opera as a joint artistic production draws on musicians, singers, set designers, directors, writers, producers, marketing and technical staff to create a spectacle for an audience. Within the landscape of opera there are different communities at work. Ellie made a conscious decision to 'punch' her way into opera:

> I was at a point in my career where I could play multiple roles as 'the artist'. I already had an interest in music having studied classical oboe and piano at school. The language of music was therefore familiar to me. I could follow a score in rehearsal and understood stage directions. I was able to imagine what my role in opera might be, partly based on well-known artists who had made this transition before; famously David Hockney, Anish Kapoor and Bill Viola. A model of 'artist in opera' already existed so I felt comfortable 'persuading' this new community that I had a valid place in their world.
>
> I often felt incapable, unfamiliar with specific vocabulary and ignorant about the infrastructure of opera. Retrospectively, I see that the obstacles I encountered working in opera were as much about my imagined lack of legitimacy – 'I'm not a real musician' – as they were in the way others perceived me. Other obstacles were simply characteristic of the hierarchy of opera, different from Fine Art or Education.

When infiltrating a new community of practice you must be flexible enough to adapt to different frameworks and working patterns but also remain true to your 'core' identity. Maintaining your own definable characteristics is important. These attributes maintain your identity and make you creatively desirable to another community of practice.

When it comes to Alison and the art world and Ellie and the world of education and opera, they are not full participants. They dabble around the edges participating in a narrow spectrum of activities. Their stories reflect the way in which a peripheral member of a community of practice can have a significant connection to it. Even those who rarely or never visit may see themselves belonging in ways exceeding their degree of actual involvement. This connection reflects an identity position of *imagination with peripheral engagement.*

Alison helps students become fine artists though she herself only tinkers around the edge of the world of art. With imagination as incorporating past membership of communities of practice (Kanno and Norton 2003), Alison's history as an art student and teacher provides her with an empathy and connection to artists. Empathy as the ability to transpose oneself into the internal frame of reference, emotions and meanings of others without ever losing yourself (Gallo 1994), is an act of imagination. These acts of imagination enable Alison to maintain a peripheral position in the art world but maintain the strong sense of connection, commitment and alignment to it that supports her work and legitimacy as an educational manager.

Ellie is a professional visitor travelling across the landscape in a number of temporary and peripheral roles. Imagination incorporates recognizing our own experience as reflecting broader patterns, connections and configurations (Wenger 1998). Other artists can be *imagined* by Ellie as living similar lives of peripheral engagement in different settings. The notion of paradigmatic trajectories in particular highlights the role of identification resting on imagining others' careers. A paradigmatic trajectory is a model trajectory embodied formally through things such as career ladders as well as the practices of people in a community of practice who model the legitimacy of this form of participation (Wenger 1998). For Ellie, her peripheral role in art education is a common practice in a setting where the legitimacy of the educator depends upon their multimembership – that is, working as a practising artist. Ellie punching her way into the opera world suggests that this paradigmatic trajectory is less well developed though some artists have demonstrated to her that this pathway is possible.

Like Alison, Ellie's comfort with her peripheral engagement is partly grounded in her history. Her family life in a pedagogical environment supports her identification with teaching. Although her background in studying music provides Ellie with the interactional expertise (Edwards 2010) necessary for peripheral engagement, she feels uncomfortable in the operatic world as she is unfamiliar with the vocabulary and infrastructure. While Ellie's peripheral involvement with the educational and operatic world seems ambivalent, it is very different in nature to Sheila's sense of displacement. Unlike Sheila, whose strong identification with academia hindered her connection with the leadership programme, Ellie's 'core' identity as a practising artist has the opposite effect. Being steeped in artistic practices provides her with a strong sense of legitimacy because wherever she is, the value she brings is as an outsider connected to the world 'out there' which in itself enables her to infuse her contribution with insight and creativity.

Managing hybrid identities

We are not born with complex identities. We become multiplied through our trajectory across the landscape. These stories highlight that identity and knowledgeability is best understood not as a function of participation in a single community of practice but in terms of multimembership. People have hybrid identities. Connections across the landscape can be durable and remain significant over long periods of time. It is not necessarily so that organizational socialization is losing its significance (Franco and Tavares 2013) or that practitioners identify lightly with the contemporary workplace (Sennett 1998). These practitioners feel accountable to various regimes of competence across the landscape even if they are no longer participating members.

Furthermore, identity is much more nuanced than 'identifying' or not 'identifying' with a practice. As this chapter suggests, it is a multifaceted construct. It changes and evolves. Sometimes identification lags behind participation and at other times helps orient practitioners to their circumstances. Although settings vary in the kinds of identifications they allow, practitioners do not passively acquiesce. They 'talk back' (Lomax 2013), trying to change their circumstances modulating their identities by identifying in one mode and not others. They may engage in strategic moves to maintain productive multimembership. People may reflexively find ways to maintain some form of identification that allows congruence with their multimembership. Identity does not necessarily fragment but rather the individual strives to maintain personal coherence (Billett and Pavlova 2005).

In understanding learning and practice, considering an individual's participation as contained within a single setting overlooks the importance of personal identification with communities of practice across the landscape. Thorpe and Mayes (2009) suggest that educators should construct learning tasks that have resonance with student practices outside their immediate setting. For learners unable to identify with the learning goals presented, facilitating their development may require that the educator bring to bear the resources of empathy, insight and persuasion needed to encourage learners to see things differently. Considering Sheila, for example, an empathic and perceptive mentor may have found ways to tap into her personal commitment to improve leadership practice and encourage her engagement.

Thorpe and Mayes (2009) also note that understanding identity as a function of multimembership may elude conventional methods such as testing or evaluation. They suggest that the educator may choose to take on the mantle of the ethnographer, researching the cultural backgrounds of the learners, their view of themselves and their purposes. Given that understanding and managing identity is also a role for managers and leaders (Lomax 2013), such an approach may be of value there too. The task here is challenging but in terms of enabling people to fully identify and learn, it may well be worth the effort.

References

Billett, S. and Pavlova, M. (2005). Learning through working life: self and individuals' agentic action. *International Journal of Lifelong Education* 24(3): 195–211.

Burt, R. S. (2000). The network structure of social capital. In R. I. Sutton and B. M. Staw, *Research in Organizational Behaviour*. Greenwich, CT, JAI Press, pp. 345–423.

Church, M., Bitel, M., Armstrong, K., Fernando, P., Gould, H., Joss, S., Marwaha-Diedrich, M., de la Torre, A. L. and Vouhe, C. (2003). *Participation, Relationships and Dynamic Change: New Thinking on Evaluating the Work of International Networks*. London, University College London.

Edwards, A. (2010). *Being an Expert Professional Practitioner: The Relational Turn in Expertise*. Dordrecht, Springer.

Franco, M. and Tavares, P. (2013). The influence of professional identity on the process of nurses' training: an empirical study. *Leadership in Health Services* 26(2): 118–134.

Gallo, D. (1994). Educating for empathy, reason and imagination. In K. S. Walters, *Re-Thinking Reason: New Perspectives in Critical Thinking*. Albany, State University of New York Press, pp. 43–60.

Hodges, D. C. (1998). Participation as dis-identification with/in a community of practice. *Mind, Culture & Activity* 5(4): 272–290.

Jarvis, P. (2006). *Towards a Comprehensive Theory of Human Learning*. Abingdon, Routledge.

Kanno, Y. and Norton, B. (2003). Imagined communities and educational possibilities: introduction. *Journal of Language, Identity and Education* 24(2): 241–249.

Lomax, H. (2013). Managing identities. In S. MacKian and J. Simons, *Leading, Managing, Caring: Understanding Leadership and Management in Health and Social Care*. Abingdon, Routledge, pp. 139–164.

Niez, T. (2010). Chasms and bridges: generativity in the space between educators' communities of practice. *Teaching and Teacher Education* 26(1): 37–44.

Sennett, R. (1998). *The Corrosion of Character: The Personal Consequences of Work in the New Capitalism*. London, Norton.

Shain, F. and Gleeson, D. (1999). Under new management: changing conceptions of teacher professionalism and policy in the further education sector. *Journal of Education Policy* 14(4): 445–462.

Solomon, Y. J. (2007). Not belonging? What makes a functional learner identity in undergraduate mathematics? *Studies in Higher Education* 32(1): 79–96.

Thorpe, M. and Mayes, T. (2009). The implications of learning contexts for pedagogical practice. In R. Edwards, G. Biesta and M. Thorpe, *Rethinking Contexts for Learning and Teaching: Communities, Activities and Networks*. Abingdon, Routledge, pp. 149–161.

Unwin, L., Fuller, A., Felstead, A. and Jewson, N. (2009). Worlds within worlds: the relational dance between context and pedagogy in the workplace. In R. Edwards, G. Biesta and M. Thorpe, *Rethinking Contexts for Learning and Teaching: Communities, Activities and Networks*. London, Routledge, pp. 106–118.

Wenger, E. (1998). *Communities of Practice: Learning, Meaning, and Identity*. Cambridge, Cambridge University Press.

Chapter 5

Brokering boundary encounters

Chris Kubiak, Mark Fenton-O'Creevy,
Karen Appleby, Maxine Kempster, Michael Reed,
Carla Solvason and Mary Thorpe

In chapter one, Etienne and Bev argued that knowledgeability is more than competence within a single community of practice. Knowledgeability reflects a person's connection with a multiplicity of practices across the landscape. Educators aiming to develop knowledgeable practitioners might organize learning programmes in which students engage with a range of practices from the landscape. They may draw in a range of resources from outside the academy – research material, policy documents or case material, for example. Visiting speakers such as practitioners or service users may reflect important parts of the landscape. Ellie and Alison's story in Chapter four is one such example. Their fine arts programme included a course taught by a visiting artist who helped students understand the practicalities of a working life in the fine arts. Educators may also create opportunities for learners to engage in learning activities in different parts of the landscape. For example, many courses require students to take workplace placements as part of their study.

Developing knowledgeability involves facilitating cross-boundary learning experiences. Facilitating such experiences often involves brokering. As Burt (2005) and Wenger (1998) both explain, brokers work at the boundaries of the landscape building connections between different practices, introducing practices from elsewhere and facilitating cross-boundary experiences. Brokers strive to support boundary crossing by facilitating the translation, coordination and alignment of different perspectives and meanings (Wenger, 1998).

This chapter explores the role of brokering in creating learning experiences by focusing on three questions:

What is it that brokers do to facilitate the development of knowledgeability? Communities of practice have particular purposes and ways of doing things which may not be shared between different parts of the landscape. Educational research is replete with examples of those in learning settings preferring to focus on their particular interests rather than incorporate concerns or practices from elsewhere. As discussed in earlier chapters, boundaries are often places of misunderstanding and confusion. Crossing a boundary or introducing an idea from elsewhere in the landscape can result in feelings of inadequacy, personal failure or disengagement. What brokering processes and skills are involved in enabling successful cross-boundary encounters or reflection on practices from elsewhere in the landscape?

How do boundary objects support boundary encounters and enable points of connection? Boundary objects enable collaborative working and sharing of practice across the landscape. They facilitate communication and coordination by providing a structure to align activity which is meaningful to all involved (Oborn & Dawson, 2010). For example, a blueprint is a boundary object which enables the different occupational groups involved in construction to plan and coordinate their actions (Star, 2010). Similarly, the Network Learning Communities programme introduced the 'levels of learning' model to provide schools, universities and local authorities with a shared language and frame of reference to plan together and share practice (Hadfield, 2005). There are different types of boundary objects – standardized forms for sharing information between organizations, libraries, maps, common languages, concepts, theories and models of the world (Benn et al., 2013). However, a key characteristic is that they are flexible enough to be interpreted in terms of the particular needs of specific groups (Star, 2010). So, although a blueprint is an overall plan, an electrician, a carpenter or an interior decorator will not use it in the same way or for the same purposes. The boundary object supports connection and collaboration but does not force consensus of meaning.

How do brokers build the legitimacy of their activities? Communities of practice are often focused on their own processes, aims and regime of competence. This means that those working at the boundaries and attempting to draw attention to matters elsewhere in the landscape may be seen as lacking legitimacy. While brokers perceived as 'one of us' are more likely to win the trust of the community of practice, those seen as 'outsiders' may be seen as clumsy, rude or intrusive (Burt, 2000). Even if enough of an 'insider' to have the legitimacy to be listened to, they must also remain outward facing so as to offer a different perspective which provides value to the community of practice (Wenger, 1998). As such, a broker may need to remain at the edge of the community of practice, a liminal inside-outsider constantly faced with the challenge of how to make the practice of one community of practice relevant to another.

In the four stories that follow, we return to these three questions to explore how facilitating learning in a landscape of practice involves brokering boundary encounters. Our discussion begins with Maxine's story.

Practice education

Maxine Kempster is a programme tutor supporting, guiding and monitoring students through a four-year pre-registration nursing programme. Her students take a number of workplace placements intended to develop the Nursing and Midwifery Council's (NMC) proficiencies. Maxine liaises between the students, their workplace mentors and the university. She makes sure that students access the right sort of experience, establishing learning goals that will provide direction for future learning and supporting the development of a portfolio of evidence needed for assessment against the NMC proficiencies. She also provides pastoral support to students and practical advice to help mentors assess practice. She sees herself facilitating learning but she does not teach students directly. She supports the mentors in their assessment role and guides students in the preparation of their portfolio but she does not assess students herself.

Maxine's story

I am the link between the university and the practice area. I work from home, at a distance from both the academic centre and the practice areas, so, in both a geographical as well as a professional sense I occupy a space between the two. I maintain contact with my students through e-mail and by telephone but much of my work involves meeting students in the placement setting, often informally, to make contact or perhaps discuss issues of current concern. However, the really in-depth work takes place during the more formal pre-scheduled meetings with the student and their mentor.

In these meetings we review the students' portfolios, including records of practice hours, experience and evidence to support the students' achievement of the NMC proficiencies. The mentor and student work together during the relevant practice period and the discussion is designed to bring out and record what they have achieved, as assessed by the mentor. Learning needs can then be identified and learning opportunities planned to meet these, culminating in a summative discussion meeting where the mentor judges whether the student has achieved the NMC proficiencies.

These discussions can be anxiety provoking for all concerned, especially early on in the programme when the participants may be unfamiliar with each other. Students may be anxious about 'being assessed', needing to gather evidence and adapting to the student role. The mentor may be pressed for time and anxious about the judgements they need to make. I might be anxious about being in an unfamiliar environment and how I am viewed by both mentor and student. Am I seen as an outsider, a visiting academic, out of touch with the realities of practice? Or am I seen as a credible practitioner who understands workplace issues?

Clearly, discussions conducted in an atmosphere of anxiety are unlikely to be productive; therefore, developing relationships in which open discussion can take place is crucial. Relationships with students usually develop quite quickly but can take longer with practice-based staff. I can break down barriers by discussing my own experiences as a nurse and a ward manager in similar care settings. I try to get a 'feel' for staff concerns and issues in each workplace. In this way, staff may begin to accept me as a fellow nurse and not as a total outsider. I do recognize though that becoming too close would compromise my role.

Students need to link course ideas and frameworks to workplace practices. They can find this difficult as they may see the two as separate or mismatched. They may also have difficulties articulating how their day-to-day work relates to the NMC proficiencies, as these tend to use unfamiliar language and concepts. Abstract terms such as ethics or equity, for example, can be difficult to relate to what may be regarded as basic or routine practice. Part of my role therefore, is to clarify these concepts using language which both the student and mentor can easily understand and relate to. Once again, I use my own experience as examples.

Here's an example. The student's portfolio needs to show that they have evidence of meeting the patients' nutritional needs. One student found this difficult to achieve in her mental health placement. However, when we discussed her recent experience she described an older patient with both an eating disorder and dementia. She'd found it difficult coordinating his care. My main task here was to enable the student to reflect on the care she delivered, and appreciate its complexities in both an academic and practice-based sense. She'd done a lot that was clearly relevant to the NMC proficiencies – liaising with specialist services and the patient's family; researching the issues; and drawing up and implementing a care plan with the patient, family and staff. She just needed help to see this.

In the discussion we interrogated the experience drawing on resources from the placement, such as local policies and assessment documentation. The mentor and I shared similar experiences. Particularly important for the student were her difficulties in obtaining specialist advice from another team who were unwilling to support a patient with dementia and in delegating to a healthcare assistant reluctant to accept her leadership. It was important that the student felt that the meeting was a safe space in which to discuss these issues.

Our discussion helped the student to develop a comprehensive piece of evidence for her portfolio which reflected the learning activity and enabled her to tell her story. This meant that the evidence went beyond nutritional aspects of care by illustrating the student's advocacy for the patient and her developing confidence in working with and delegating to her team.

Maxine facilitates a boundary encounter that connects academic study, the NMC's proficiencies and workplace experience in order to develop the student's knowledgeability. Although the example of nutrition appears focused on providing evidence for the portfolio, it is primarily a learning process in which nursing is viewed within a landscape of practice which extends beyond the placement. As a result, the student reframes her practice experience in terms of academic ideas and the NMC proficiencies.

In terms of brokering, two processes are relevant here. First, establishing a micro-climate of trust is important to brokering (Church et al., 2003; Kerr et al., 2003). Maxine does not want to be seen as a threat; meeting in an atmosphere of anxiety would not be productive. Trust takes time to build because it emerges out of relationships with some shared history (the informal contacts Maxine mentions, for example) in which individuals build a stake in maintaining a reputation for honesty and reliability (Fukuyama, 1995). Without trusting relationships, the anxiety and uncertainty associated with this role may inhibit learning.

Second, brokering involves more than drawing together different types of information. Maxine helps the student articulate her experience, translating and aligning this to the requirements of the academy and the NMC. The NMC proficiencies and the portfolio are boundary objects which act as a tangible bridge between the NMC, the academy and the placement (Harris et al., 2001). They define who needs to be involved in the encounter. They provide a shared focus and framework for the discussion which supports the process of aligning and interpreting practice experience. These are flexible boundary objects which serve several purposes:[1] organizing evidence, assessing performance, providing a paper trail, focusing discussion, setting learning goals and planning for further development. Serving several purposes helps these boundary objects make connections between different practices.

Even with a basis of trust, established relationships and boundary objects, Maxine needs to build legitimacy. Working at the periphery of the academy and the workplace, she takes care to build relationships with the mentors and understand the issues in their workplace. Lack of relationships or understanding could undermine her legitimacy as a broker and leave others doubting the relevance or value of her contribution. She consciously works on impression management (Goffman, 1959) by getting a feel for each workplace's issues and evoking her practice experience. Her aim is to present not as a naive out-of-touch visitor but as someone qualified to discuss nursing.

Maxine's story illustrates that brokering involves working with the emotional as well as instrumental aspects of supporting the development of knowledgeability. In the next story, Mary Thorpe, a Professor of Educational Technology at the Open University, describes brokering a learning experience that reflected the landscape of practice. She was, however, working at a much greater scale.

Developing learning resources for the practice setting

The Open University (OU) offers free and paid-for courses and resources delivered through open and distance learning methods. In Mary Thorpe's story, she describes the creation of a professional development website for practising social workers. The website, which can be seen as a boundary object, was created by mobilizing various resources from across the landscape and brokering a number of boundary encounters.

Mary's story

Our website offers users learning activities focusing on video clips of social work practice. As the clips originate from a television series made with the BBC, we encountered our first challenge. Permission from each person featured is needed before we can reuse the clips. We trip over the boundaries between two organizations. Although these resources are owned by both the OU and the BBC, we do not share a common understanding of what is in the public interest. But we discover a hidden resource – ongoing working relationships between the OU academics in our team and the social workers from the original filming. The social workers willingly provide permission. They also contact the service users originally featured in the series whose permissions we also need. This good will enables us to overcome a hurdle that could have prevented us using the video material altogether. We make small payments to the service users featured in the clips, but the policy is that social workers can't receive anything. We can't show our gratitude to practitioners who have given their time in both small and large ways over the whole process. This reminds us how the Open University and its staff often rely on goodwill from many practitioners who are not part of our organization. Our goals are not their goals but because we are about learning and helping people change their lives through study, we can generate and benefit from these shared broad values that play a silent role in our interactions.

If we remain solely within our organizational boundaries, we risk launching a site that makes assumptions about how social workers would use the material. So we start to work at the boundaries of our organization. We invite colleagues in our regional centres to give us contacts with social work employers who can tell us what they want from a professional development website. We launch the site through demonstration workshops with social work team leaders. They see the site's potential to complement their existing staff development work but once they view the video clips, their engagement immediately increases. The video clips offer something that local training cannot and they immediately suggest a range of potential uses and users within each organization. Making contact with social work employers has paid off with the realization that the video material is in demand and our vision of potential use expands. Team leaders want to use the video clips during group meetings to spark discussion of social work issues. We had originally seen the site as individual-focused, but feedback suggested that group learning may be as important. So we add a new area to the site, where all video clips are available as free-standing items for providers to view for whatever purpose they wish and in any order they choose. They also ask us to provide more resources on social work with adults not just children. We start to commission a new set of resources that are text-based but cover these areas of adult services.

These contacts are energizing but initial enthusiasm doesn't always lead to an actual, viable working relationship. E-mails go unanswered. Actually, a lot of contacts just seem to fade away. Our assumptions that e-mails are read and responded to within a day or two, that decisions can be made at a distance, and that action will follow on agreements made often prove false. Even those we have met face to face may not respond despite their early interest. Is this staff turnover, sudden crisis or a thousand and one other things that we can only guess at? Moving beyond one's own organizational boundaries is hugely labour intensive, we discover. But the problem is greater than this. Even though we want to meet the needs of social workers, is it possible to establish in-depth co-working beyond a fleeting face-to-face meeting or phone conversation? How we can move beyond brief encounters in this other world and get something happening?

Through our boundary encounters we realized that while we think of social work as one practice, distinct from our own, practitioner groups are incredibly diverse and we can work more easily with some than with others. Our demonstration workshops, for example, enable us to appreciate that a sub-group within social work – practice educators – lack readily available resources to use with individual social workers on placements. They immediately see the potential use of our site in their core role. We set up an online forum for them. We contact each one individually, but we also recognize that they need to find others on our site like them, so we start to work with one or two activists who can readily work in our world and on our website, make use of its resources and forums, while also being of the social work world themselves.

These are innovators who use IT where others do not, consultants, educators or trainers. These are people who can take on some leadership. They provide an important channel of feedback that shapes the site's development. But they are also activists themselves, encouraging the use of the website among their colleagues. This means that we are accessing a different kind of feedback about the resource, one based not on discussions of intended use but on actual use.

We have worked together as a team on a vision for the site, but these meetings with employers and social work educators add something new; something that we could not have envisaged by working simply within the boundaries of our group. But we also learn that we have stepped into a very challenging environment for web-based learning. Certainly, social workers have limited time to do anything but their workplaces make it difficult to use the web. Firewalls, IT policies and hot desking all effectively block access to the internet as a routine aspect of personal practice. Some employers restrict online access to any but internal systems for records and accounting, making it impossible to use even relevant social work sites such as those hosted by the Social Care Institute for Excellence. Some employers themselves do not understand how effective ICT usage can support improved outcomes for service users. All this suggests that our project is ambitious in its expectations about how social workers will use an online site. However, our contacts suggest that we should be optimistic that old practices are changing and the use of online technology will creep into the world of social work.

Looking back, we see how our project has arisen from seeing opportunities and taking advantage of what a large organization such as the Open University offers as support for innovation. Funding and expertise from our Practice-based Professional Learning Centre of Excellence in Teaching and Learning enabled us to buy out the time of the people needed to build the site. We had a tight schedule which demands that we work flexibly and responsively between ourselves and also tried to cut through hold-ups by persistence and friendly pushing of colleagues whose contributions, as in the negotiations with the BBC, have been pivotal. Perhaps again it's the values of the wider organization that pull us all together – both our immediate team and our wider set of contacts in the organization. People know we are aiming at goals that fit with our university's emphasis on 'openness as to people, places, methods and ideas'. They know we are working to a tight schedule, and they are willing to try to fit with that. They don't operate bureaucratically in other words.

We are bidding for funding to develop the site further. We need to build a new set of contacts and describe our site and why it matters, using different terminology. The project is almost chameleon-like as its audiences change. We have to move outside our own comfort zone but have to have some credibility with different audiences. We need to speak their language while retaining our core vision.

Mary's brokering involves mobilizing human and material resources from across the landscape to create a website. The site's production involves an array of cross-boundary encounters. She engages with academics, social workers and service users as well as the BBC to gain access to documentary material. She draws on networks with Open University regional staff to make contact with social work team leaders to plan the site. She draws in social work 'activists' to work on the site and encourage other practitioners to use it. Mary is a broker working a network of networks. This network is not defined by organizational boundaries but interdependencies, shared histories, goodwill and relationships.

Mary's work resonates with Trevillion's (1999) description of brokers in social work as spiders spinning a web of individuals from different organizations or gathering together resources in order to address a specific need. The ability to pull together others who know the territory, have influence and relationships has been described as 'know who' (Edwards et al., 2010: 31). Using 'know who' helps build the project's legitimacy in that it involves finding ways into the landscape through other 'boundary creatures' such as activist social workers or regional colleagues. These people already work, and have legitimacy, within the social work and educational worlds. After all, changing learning habits across the landscape has to involve the people located there. The routines of practice are not readily changed by outsiders.

The web Mary spins runs across different teams, departments and organizations. Each community of practice operates with its own goals, routines, language and conventions. These create a boundary when it comes to legitimately introducing a new website into practice. If the boundaries between each practice were thought of as physical boundaries, blocking access to another practice, they vary in height. The boundaries created by the different terminology used by funding bodies can be lowered through her multilingualism. The boundaries imposed by the bureaucratic requirements to obtain permission are lowered by the relationships with people on the other side. However, the highest boundary seems to lie between Mary and the social work world. Contacts become unresponsive. This world of practice has a different regime of accountability, commitments and repertoires. Mary's way of working – e-mail, extended conversations about learning needs, collaborative planning – does not resonate in this environment and she can only just penetrate the periphery.

Mary's brokering also incorporates visionary boundary objects. Visionary boundary objects are concepts or visions with a high degree of legitimacy in that they resonate emotionally with people within particular communities of practice and are therefore difficult to oppose (Briers & Chua, 2001). Mary overcomes the problems of misalignment by appealing to concerns common to both education and social work; those of helping people and improving lives. Sharing a purpose helps groups move from a position of 'us' and 'them' to 'we' and in doing so, transcend problematic boundaries. The common values generate good will from the social workers, who help Mary get the permission she needs to use the video. Common values hold her disparate team together and motivate them to side-step the limitations of organizational bureaucracy.

Mary's brokering involved mobilizing informational, financial, organizational and human resources to create a learning opportunity for social workers. She uses 'know who' to spin a web of contacts who shape the project and build its legitimacy. Her use of visionary boundary objects helps her build support for the project across the landscape. The next story also focuses on a team of educators encouraging practitioners to look beyond their usual work practice to support students on a foundation degree.

Creating the team around the student on a Foundation Degree for Early Years Practitioners

Students on the Foundation Degree for Early Years Practitioners take a number of work-based courses which require them to straddle the boundary between the workplace and the university. The tutors Karen Appleby, Michael Reed and Carla Solvason decided to directly address the boundary issues at play by involving local authority advisors in providing student support.

The tutors' story

We wanted to support the different aspects of the students' learning needs. We already supported their studies through academic tutors. Personal tutors attended to their wellbeing. However, because these tutors focused more on academic outcomes we felt that the learning process could become rather insular rather than one concerned with real practice and workplace improvements. We wanted someone to work with students in the workplace to help them focus on these wider outcomes. The local authority advisors were ideal for this role. After all, they had a sound understanding and knowledge of the students' settings.

So we met with the Workforce Development Lead to discuss a role for the local authority in supervising students. Approval gave us the authority to pull together a series of Partnership Forum Meetings with advisors from different local authorities, their managers and university staff. We didn't approach them with a specific proposal or statement of what we wanted done. We had not identified a particular task that we wanted carried out. These meetings were based on a concern with mutual appeal. That is, how can we best support the practitioners on our programme to improve outcomes for the children in their care? It was out of this concern that we wanted the vision to emerge.

There was a fair bit of reshuffling of roles in the first couple of meetings. We wanted the approach to student support to emerge out of the discussion but it took a while for the advisors to feel confident that they could genuinely contribute to this agenda. This was partly because we worked in such different ways and we needed to find common ground. Even so, looking back on the notes we took in the meeting we could see that there was a lot of enthusiasm for the partnership. Here are some excerpts:

> It's about changing hearts and minds. Consultant's impact will be vital. It's about the children. Consultants have to engage with the process.
>
> Local authority senior staff

> We need to ensure that the FdA [Foundation Degree] is not divorced from settings . . . the students need to be able to show what is making a difference, individually and within settings. Making 'real evidence' rather than just putting in to pass an assignment.
>
> University manager

Even with this good will and enthusiasm, we hit a deadlock over the title the advisors would take. After a lot of discussion the advisors decided that 'Professional Practice Consultant' best encompassed the role they saw themselves developing. By toying with different titles – 'professional partner, facilitator, improvement guide, coach, advisor' – we were doing more than coming up with the right words. It was a discussion about 'who we are', 'what we do' and our responsibilities. Pinning these issues down was important because students needed to be clear on which issues are taken to their university tutor and which should go to the advisors.

Discussing titles sorted out who does what and why. As a result, agendas were constructed, discussion took place, committees were consulted, documents drafted and proposals made. As well as sorting out roles, this discussion of words, roles and responsibilities helped us better understand the advisors' perception of the issues. We finished the process with a deeper sense of trust in one another's motives.

So the advisors started working with students. However, some didn't quite have the focus on supporting practice development that we had hoped. There was a fair bit of 'Mother Henning' going on where the advisors focused on the students' emotional and personal issues. These discussions with students were important for developing strong supportive relationships but they didn't progress the students far in terms of the development of their practice. We assured the advisors that the students' personal tutors would provide pastoral support – this need would not go unmet. The advisors did get the message and they gave more attention to practice development. Even so, some 'Mother Henning' remained. This role would always be there.

Looking back, we feel that we have all changed. We academics gave away our authority as we brought in others better able to support students in practice development. The advisors became more familiar with our teaching materials and they felt more comfortable telling us what they thought about them. This has been invaluable feedback on how our teaching materials transferred to practice contexts. As important though, this enthusiasm and critique reflected how engaged the advisors had become with our project.

The students in this story are straddling the workplace–academy boundary. Their academic development is well attended to but, when it comes to the other side of the boundary, improvement of practice has been neglected. To ensure that the students' learning is truly a cross-boundary experience, they enlist the help of those from the students' practice world, the local authority advisors, to support practice improvement.

Legitimacy is an important aspect of this story. The tutors take the well-established route of seeking permission from management. Although broker-ing cross-institutional partnerships can appear to exist outside of normal institutional processes (Edwards et al., 2010), authority structures still play a significant role. As with Mary's story, the legitimacy of the tutors' work is also derived from a purpose common to both parties: a concern with improving outcomes for children. This common purpose sustains the participants over the several meetings needed to establish a concrete plan. Even so, the boundary encounter is precarious. Open-ended discussions have the potential to be inconclusive while a lack of openness to the concerns of those involved may be alienating.

The foundation degree tutors want to change the roles and working practices of a staff group in another organization. The skill required here relates to an observation made by Lieberman and Grolnick (1996) in their discussion of school-to-school learning networks: brokers need to articulate possible ways forward, allow actions to emerge out of the group and secure commitment by negotiating around intellectual, ideological and practical differences. Such work requires a light touch. Trying to control things too much can drain initiative and strangle the dynamism of the people involved while having too light a structure can place undue pressure on the trust between participants (Kerr et al., 2003).

Deciding on a title for the advisors can be read as the creation of a boundary object that would resonate with the academics, the advisors and the students. Discussing the meaning of different words grounds the participants' understandings of how people across the landscape see things. Also, the very need for a title reflects the nature of the landscape itself. Titles are important there. Organizations celebrate them or use them to assign responsibility and status. Professionals expect to have them. Titles establish legitimacy. Ultimately, the title holds the academic–advisor partnership together by encapsulating the commitments, agreements and expectations of the parties involved. Donning the title is an act of accepting these intangible responsibilities and becomes a sign that one is an agenda holder.

This story of brokering describes legitimacy as based in both institutional authority (permission to work together) and the moral authority of a fundamental professional purpose. Brokering focused on bringing about role change takes time and must be exercised with openness and a light touch. Finally, the creation of a boundary object with resonance across the landscape is a productive means of establishing the character of the work.

All the stories so far have described the process of building legitimacy. Without legitimacy, neither the broker nor boundary encounter will be able to achieve much. The last story in this chapter describes the uncertainty of working when legitimacy is in doubt.

Convening networks in the pharmaceutical business

Michelle is employed by a pharmaceutical company.[2] She organizes and facilitates a number of European expert networks aiming to improve the lives of patients and families by improving the diagnosis and treatment of a specific group of diseases. The networks exchange information, make sense of situations and share developments in drug treatments. In recent years, Michelle has felt a growing sense that the purposes of the networks and those of her employer are in conflict.

Michelle's story

Each expert in the network represents a regional or national specialist centre. These networks have a fairly broad membership crossing country and professional boundaries. Membership diversity also brings diversity of goals and values. It is important for each stakeholder in the network or community to subscribe to a strong common mission and values – a common focus on improving the lives of patients and families. I am passionate about this work and its value. Just as well. To have any credibility in these networks I need to share their values.

Over time, the networks have maintained a stable culture and climate, whilst the company has changed ownership and management. This change has caused some instability and uncertainty. With all this change going on, I have more of a sense of belonging to the stable climate of the expert network. Sometimes I feel like an outsider defending the interests of the network over the company. It's a vulnerable position to be in.

So, my role convening these networks creates tensions. I'm accountable for delivering value to the company from its investment in these networks. It's difficult because the values of the expert networks are entirely intangible whilst the company has a very tangible goal of making a profit. Even so, the company needs to maintain its responsibility towards patients – a 'hard moral' principle of doing the right thing because this is what internal and external stakeholders expect, given the nature of the business. The business can't simply be about making a profit.

However, CEOs have great difficulty in bridging the gap between intangible and tangible value. From a company's perspective they may not see a direct return. Therefore, there can be a gap between what I do and company perception of benefit. I think I'm sitting on an invaluable asset but feeling alone.

I was ill for a while and had to take a lot of time off work. I felt even more vulnerable. But then I changed the way I saw things. I was working on a part-time MBA. Completing it left me with a much stronger sense of my employability. I realized that I would still thrive if I left my current organization. This gave me the confidence to be much clearer about my values in relation to the networks and my own worth to both networks and company. I think in many ways this has led to the company valuing me more.

Michelle is facilitating a network which runs across the landscape of practice way beyond the boundaries of her organization. While the other stories describe the process of initiating boundary encounters of this kind, Michelle describes the workings of a much more mature network. These groups with their stable cultures and well-established purposes give rise to a particular kind of problem – competing regimes of accountability. The moral focus, intangible values and long-term returns associated with this network sit uncomfortably with the company's focus on the bottom line as a measure of value. Furthermore, the horizontal accountability of the networks' members to each other is important to hold it together but is competing with the demands of Michelle's vertical accountability to her employer. This position makes her claim to competence and legitimacy in the pharmaceutical company somewhat precarious. Others have noted that facilitating boundary encounters between practitioners from across the landscape can require rule bending because this process sits awkwardly within the procedures of the host organization's requirements (Edwards et al., 2010). Michelle's story highlights the vulnerability of brokers as her opportunity to operate outside of her employer's core purposes and measures of success appears to be dissipating as the organization evolves.

Although Michelle experiences considerable difficulties straddling the boundary between the networks and her organization, her experience on the MBA emphasizes how boundary encounters can also reinforce practitioner identity. Studying for an MBA connects her to a community with which she has strongly identified, bolstering her sense of value and improving her ability to articulate what she has to offer. This boundary encounter offers her a sense of personal value unavailable within her company and is important to building a sense of competence that may transfer to other settings across the landscape.

In conclusion then, Michelle's brokering is characterized by precarious legitimacy arising out of the competing regimes of accountability between her networks and her organization. Her vulnerability is made bearable though by a different kind of boundary encounter – the MBA programme – which builds her sense of competence and career options elsewhere.

Challenges of brokering

This chapter has presented four stories of brokering. Boundary encounters are not easily constructed and can be fraught with potential misalignments and contradictions. Boundary objects may help with aligning and coordinating perspectives. The different boundary objects discussed (titles, proficiency frameworks, portfolios, purposes and values) underscore the importance of remaining open to their different forms. The experiences of foundation degree lecturers suggest that there is value in constructing boundary objects as part of establishing the boundary encounter.

The boundary object should not be confused with the participation in the boundary encounter itself. While a boundary object may align activity or, even as Maxine found, afford access to a setting, it is only a tool to support engagement. Despite possessing well-developed boundary objects, participants still needed to carefully manage the encounter. Moreover, they may find themselves in a position of uncertain legitimacy as experienced by both Mary and Michelle.

The brokers in these stories appear to exercise considerable skill and determination in establishing the boundary encounters and driving change in the landscape. However, their capacity to bring about change arises out of shared action. Working with others in a non-authoritarian fashion, remaining open to collective will, reshaping the purposes and processes to suit the group all reflect the way that brokers give away their power in favour of collective agency. This is not to say that brokers do not require personal strength. Brokers often work in a difficult position which demands considerable personal resilience. This highlights an area of silence in these stories. What support was available to these conveners? Is there something akin to a community of brokers (Wenger, 1998)? After all, having access to the community in the MBA was extremely helpful to Michelle.

The work of brokering is challenging and at times frustrating but at no point did it appear unrewarding. After all, these brokers were dealing with work involving a strong moral purpose – a concern with changing lives, caring for the sick or educating children. These purposes, which provided the glue for the boundary encounters, were in themselves a powerful source of motivation and reward.

Notes

1. Star (2010: 4) refers to this quality as 'interpretive flexibility'.
2. Michelle is a pseudonym. The author of this story does not wish to be identified.

References

Benn, S., Edwards, M., & Angus-Leppan, T. (2013). Organizational learning and the sustainability community of practice: the role of boundary objects. *Organization & Environment, 26*(2), 184–202. doi: 10.1177/1086026613489559

Briers, M. & Chua, W. F. (2001). The role of actor-networks and boundary objects in management accounting change: a field study of an implementation of activity-based costing. *Accounting Organizations and Society, 26*(3), 237–269.

Burt, R. S. (2000). The network structure of social capital. In R. I. Sutton & B. M. Staw (Eds), *Research in Organizational Behaviour* (pp. 345–423). Greenwich, CT: JAI Press.

Burt, R. S. (2005). *Brokerage and Closure: An Introduction to Social Capital.* Oxford: Oxford University Press.

Church, M., Bitel, M., Armstrong, K., Fernando, P., Gould, H., Joss, S., Vouhe, C., et al. (2003). *Participation, Relationships and Dynamic Change: New Thinking on Evaluating the Work of International Networks.* London: University College London.

Edwards, A., Lunt, I., & Stamou, E. (2010). Inter-professional work and expertise: new roles at the boundaries of schools. *British Educational Research Journal, 36*(1), 27–45. doi: 10.1080/01411920902834134

Fukuyama, F. (1995). *Trust: The Social Virtues and the Creation of Prosperity.* New York: Free Press.

Goffman, E. (1959). *The Presentation of Self in Everyday Life.* New York: Anchor.

Hadfield, M. (2005). From networking to school networks to 'networked' learning: the challenge for the Networked Learning Communities Programme. In W. Veugelers & M. J. O'Hair (Eds), *Network Learning for Educational Change* (pp. 172–191). Maidenhead: Open University Press.

Harris, S., Dolan, G., & Fairbairn, G. (2001). Reflecting on the use of student portfolios. *Nurse Education Today, 21*(4), 278–286. doi: http://dx.doi.org/10.1054/nedt.2000.0545

Kerr, D., Aiston, S., White, K., Holland, M., & Grayson, H. (2003). *Review of Networked Learning Communities.* Slough: NFER.

Lieberman, A. & Grolnick, M. (1996). Networks and reform in American education. *Teacher's College Record, 98*(1), 1–44.

Oborn, E. & Dawson, S. (2010). Learning across communities of practice: an examination of multidisciplinary work. *British Journal of Management, 21*(4), 843–858. doi: 10.1111/j.1467-8551.2009.00684.x

Star, S. L. (2010). This is not a boundary object: reflections on the origin of a concept. *Science, Technology & Human Values, 35*(5), 601–617. doi: 10.1177/0162243910377624

Trevillion, S. (1999). *Networking and Community Partnership.* Aldershot: Ashgate Publishing Ltd.

Wenger, E. (1998). *Communities of Practice: Learning, Meaning and Identity.* Cambridge: Cambridge University Press.

Part III

Convening

In Part II we looked at landscapes of practice from the perspective of those living there. In Part III we take a different view and consider the work of people who take a 'systems' view of the landscape and who work actively to enable new learning. These 'systems conveners' act to reconfigure the landscape by forging new learning partnerships across traditional boundaries.

To bring this emerging role to life, we have invited some conveners we have worked with to contribute their voice to the conversation. We start with a chapter that introduces the concept of systems convener and its connections to the theory. Helped by the words of two systems conveners we have worked with we explore the challenges that systems conveners face, the type of work they do, and the personal characteristics they bring to their role. The two chapters that follow describe how these challenges have been addressed in two large-scale projects. The stories of these projects are told from the perspectives of the conveners in their complex landscapes.

The conveners in Part III all talk about cultivating communities of practice. So far in this book the concept of community of practice has been used analytically to explicate the structure of the landscape, its practices, and its boundaries. For conveners, however, communities of practice are primarily interventions in the landscape. Along with networks, projects, conversations, and relationship building, communities of practice are ways for conveners to forge new learning partnerships, create new capabilities, and enable new identities in the landscape. When these conveners cultivate communities of practice as interventions in the landscape, they bring together people from diverse locations in order to transform practice. These people may not see each other as obvious learning partners; they may in fact come from very different or even conflicting perspectives. Helping them recognize the potential value of forming a learning partnership oriented to transforming practice usually takes work. Boundaries have to be negotiated; commonalities have to be discovered; perspectives have to be realigned; and enough trust has to be built that people can start to learn together by inspecting their practices and related boundaries. When these conveners adopt this approach, what they cultivate are indeed communities of practice – not in the simple sense of having the same practices, but in the more complex sense of forming heterogeneous learning partnerships to transform existing practices or create new practices.

Chapter 6

Systems conveners in complex landscapes

Beverly Wenger-Trayner
and Etienne Wenger-Trayner

In our role as learning consultants for different organizations we increasingly find ourselves supporting conveners in complex landscapes. Their contexts are different but what drives them is similar: a conviction that new configurations of people and activities will bring about new capabilities. These conveners see a social landscape with all its separate and related practices through a wide-angle lens; they spot opportunities for creating new learning spaces and partnerships that will bring different and often unlikely people together to engage in learning across boundaries. This chapter explores the role of these conveners, the paradoxical challenges they face, the complexity of their work, and the personal traits that seem critical to their endeavor. While our description of what they do is based on an archetype of the successful conveners we have worked with we hope they will recognize themselves in our description of what they do and realize they are not alone. We also hope that others will come to appreciate the subtleties, drive, hard work, and tensions involved. Ultimately we would like to contribute to the emergence of a discipline of convening in complex landscapes.

Systems conveners: working the landscape

Systems convener is the term we are using for people who forge new learning partnerships in complex landscapes. Our emphasis is on the systemic reconfiguring by which these types of conveners open new avenues for learning.

The concept of convening has been used in different ways. Often it refers to the gathering and facilitation of specific events, conversations, or collaboration.[1] Some organizations with a social mission now call themselves 'convening organizations.' It indicates an ideological shift from being providers of finance or expertise to being conveners of people who will work together to find innovative solutions to their common problems.[2] Our focus, however, is on *people* who act as conveners. Our experience suggests that organizations, even when they claim the label of convener, depend on individuals who take leadership in the role, sometimes in the name of the organization, and sometimes in spite of it.[3]

By calling the people we describe here 'systems conveners' we are emphasizing that their concern is more about creating lasting change across social and institutional systems than about enabling collaboration among individuals. Whatever their official job title they share an ability to see the potential for learning and action in a landscape beyond their immediate scope – and they act on it. They seek to reconfigure social systems through partnerships that exploit mutual learning needs, possible synergies, various kinds of relationships, and common goals across traditional boundaries.[4]

To appreciate the role of convener we should hear about it from the voice of those who are attempting to do it. We include the voices of two people with whom we have worked and who brought a convening approach to their endeavor. We have subsequently interviewed them about their experience. Both were well into their career and although their job title did not include systems convener, they identified strongly with the role.

> **Nancy Movall (NM)**
>
> Nancy started her career as an art teacher, became the technology coordinator in her district, and is now a Grant Manager for the state of Iowa, Area Education Agency. At the time of our interview she was coordinating the development of an eCurriculum for teachers whose students were each to have their own laptop under a new state initiative. She was bringing together teachers and curriculum leaders in a number of disciplines to develop the practices they needed in their new classroom.

> **John Hegarty (JH)**
>
> When we worked with John he was Head of the Centre for Financial Reporting Reform at the World Bank in Austria. With a background as a chartered accountant, he ran a program of accounting reform and institutional strengthening in South Central and South Eastern Europe. He took a convening approach to the task, bringing together participating countries and entities to improve the reform process across the region.

The chapter is divided into three sections. We start by describing the challenges systems conveners face, often in tension between conflicting demands. Then we frame their work in terms of reconfiguring identities with the modes of identification defined in Chapter 1. Finally we list some personal but paradoxical traits that seem to characterize people who undertake this challenge.

Convening challenges: reconfiguring complex landscapes

Systems conveners view their work, explicitly or implicitly, as an endeavor to generate new capabilities in their landscape. It is a complex learning process that involves new partnerships among diverse stakeholders. To enable this learning, they attempt to reconfigure the landscape: unlocking unexplored spaces, forging promising partnerships, building bridges, resetting boundaries, challenging established colonies, and creating new settlements.

The landscapes in which conveners operate are complex. The multiplicity of stakeholders bring to the endeavor perspectives, interests, backgrounds, affiliations, and aspirations derived from different locations and trajectories in the landscape. Here are five dimensions of this complexity:

Practices. Stakeholders across the landscape identify with a variety of unrelated, overlapping, and competing practices and their respective communities. They are accountable to different regimes of competence, histories, repertoires, artifacts, languages, worldviews, and personal relationships.

Institutions. Stakeholders engage in different practices in the landscape in the context of their various organizations, which have specific missions, projects, policies, structures, and often-complicated politics. These institutions pursue different (and sometimes competing) goals, represent different constituencies, and are under pressure to meet demands placed on them by their own stakeholder groups.

Scale. Conveners' endeavors usually cross multiple levels of scale, from the very local, to the regional, national, and in many cases international. Each level of scale represents an aspect of the problem and of the solution. Different stakeholders are invested at different levels of scale and often blame other levels for enduring difficulties. Learning processes need to cross these levels of scale.

Power. The landscape is shaped by significant differences in power among practices, groups, institutions, and even individuals. The negotiation of these differences in power to shape what is done in the landscape is a significant dynamic in the forging of new learning partnerships.

Time. Time is also a dimension of complexity in a landscape of practice. For conveners the time dimension manifests in two opposite ways:

- Shifting landscape: things are constantly changing, people move on, organizations restructure, but there needs to be coherence and continuity of focus.
- Inertia: at the same time complex systems have enough inertia that real changes in practice take a long time to become sustainable.

In dealing with these dimensions conveners need to manage factors that are usually in tension and, at times, in real conflict. The tensions inherent in a landscape can present formidable obstacles but also new opportunities to spur creativity. In either case managing them is central to the role of systems convener.

Respecting and challenging boundaries

Boundaries are inherent in landscapes of practice. They reflect the limitation of the human ability for engagement. They simplify things. They serve a purpose.

Practices, institutions, and levels of scale all create boundaries as people are involved in different enterprises. Boundaries are neither good nor bad – just a fact of life. In brokering new partnerships, conveners inevitably confront traditional and enduring boundaries. Their challenge is to get buy-in from across these boundaries, including from practitioners of various communities, their organizations, sponsors, and other potential stakeholders.

> It's about our people but we've got agencies in our State and we've got programs in our State and . . . I try to gel all of that together and make it doable for what we're trying to accomplish . . . I connect people. So it's people to people, people to agencies. You know, in our State we have an intermediate agency that supports all the schools and there's a lot going on there so I have to keep making that connection and then making the connection program to program. (NM)

Conveners learn to respect the role of boundaries, even when they seem to get in the way of quickly discovering mutual interest. It is not realistic to uproot people and enlist their participation in a completely new endeavor. In seeking new common ground conveners honor the existing accountability of stakeholders to their contexts, including regimes of competence, the agendas and expectations of organizations involved, and their own trajectory through the landscape. This respect for boundaries takes patience and persistence, but the commitment to common ground is likely to be more robust.

Creating engagement across established boundaries is also risky. Conveners need to move potential stakeholders beyond their current thinking or ways of doing things and persuade them that coming together across boundaries is worth their while. But it will only work if they convince enough of the right people to take the step.

To pursue this endeavor, conveners broker and hustle between potential stakeholders to encourage participation from people with different interests and different expectations. They enlist the support of networkers, brokers, weavers, and anyone who can contribute to the social fabric and translate across boundaries. They reframe and adapt their message to address different constituents.

Translating between personal and organizational perspectives

Not only are conveners initiating tenuous conversations at the boundaries between traditionally unlikely partners, they are also balancing the outcomes with organizational, administrative, and funding demands. The more successful they are at crossing boundaries the more they need to renegotiate their own and others' accountability to structures in their organizational contexts for sponsorship and support.

Conveners are strategic networkers who build connections and rely on the sense of accountability that comes with those relationships. But persuading people of the benefits of coming together across the landscape is not enough. Conveners also have to ensure that decision-makers in hierarchical positions appreciate what they are doing. While they set out to leverage the power of network connections they also stand accountable to organizational structures and political hierarchies. Moreover, they also have to take into consideration the accountability of people to the same types of structures in their respective organizations.

> You then have to persuade people that there are costs and benefits . . . that the inputs, outputs have a benefit to them and I think that's where you have to identify the people with different interests . . . You just have to keep everybody in the loop and keep everybody happy and balancing the care and attention that you give to the various players . . . (JH)

Compounding this challenge is that the people with the most potential in new configurations are often the busiest and most likely to have competing demands from their organization and other commitments. These other demands can easily take over from any enthusiasm for engaging in cross-boundary endeavors. To be successful, conveners need to help people translate their involvement in a new endeavor into something their organizations will understand, appreciate, and support.

> How do we keep teachers enthused . . . you know . . . they get in the middle of the school year and they kind of get bogged down and things get tense . . . (NM)

Leveraging and resisting power to include a diversity of voices

In trying to reconfigure the landscape, even in small ways, conveners will inevitably meet the political nature of the landscape as described in Chapter 1. The ability to define what matters, what counts as success, what needs doing, what is permissible, and what is considered authoritative knowledge is unevenly distributed across the landscape. To reconfigure the landscape conveners need to leverage existing sources of power to achieve their goals.

At the same time, conveners have an acute awareness of the need to involve all the voices relevant to their endeavor, including, and perhaps especially, the traditionally silent ones. They see that all practices have their own perspectives, which cannot be subsumed under another. They know that the success of their endeavor depends on practitioners representing their own voices in the

> You cannot assume that just because something was in place 3 months ago it is still in place now . . . When you get changes in one chain of command, you sometimes overlook that you really have to bring them on board from zero. And the people who were there at the earlier stages sharing the enthusiasm in the room next door – they're gone! And you cannot take for granted that the people after them automatically have the same insights. (JH)

As we grow, what of those pieces need to be reinforced, introduced to the new people who come on board? I don't think it is just as simple as to just say – hey come on board . . . (NM)

I'm . . . persuading internal stakeholders . . . seeking endorsement . . . identifying sponsors . . . demonstrating to others that we have endorsement . . . tweaking the interest . . . facilitating agreement . . . There's a balance to be struck between being optimistic and over promising and I think maybe a mistake I've made is assuming that my mandate from the Bank was a given and you manage up, you manage down, you manage sideways, you manage out, you manage in, you know. It's not always easy to keep all of the different bits in balance . . . (JH)

conversation and expressing them in ways that influence the reconfiguration of the landscape.

Conveners have to engage with power without letting it get in the way. At times they need to enlist people or institutions with the power to make things happen. Sometimes they need to protect the endeavor from interferences by those same powers.

While conveners have to leverage various sources of power it is counter-productive for their endeavor if they merely reproduce traditional power structures in their efforts to leverage them. This entails a subtle dance between acknowledging the uneven distribution of power and giving voice to different and often unheard perspectives.

Dealing with power is an area where conveners have to be very strategic about keeping the landscape view. Indeed issues of power often reflect special interests with too narrow a view. Conveners are working on behalf of the whole landscape in spite of all the pressures to listen to specific interests. They seem to have an instinct that power is something to both leverage and counteract, and that an important aspect of knowledgeability in the landscape is to recognize the full set of voices relevant to the issue at hand.

Sustaining an endeavor over the long haul

Reconfiguring a landscape is long-term work. However, time scale is a challenge because the landscape both has inertia and is constantly shifting. While trying to reconfigure a landscape amidst fast-changing times conveners are also faced with long-established practices, enduring boundaries, complex institutions that reflect disjunctions between levels of scale, and powerful stakeholders with an interest in keeping the status quo. Another reason the endeavor of conveners takes time is that it depends on progress on two fronts simultaneously:

- *progress on the domain*, i.e., on the challenges that drive the endeavor and that participants care about;
- *progress on learning*, i.e., on people's understanding of learning in cross-boundary partnerships and thus on their adaptation to new ways of working.

Sustaining coherence across shifting contexts. While there is inertia in the landscape, there is also constant change. The building of alliances takes place amid shifting parameters. With tensions across multiple boundaries, the often-fragile sense of coherence conveners create among stakeholders with different interests is frequently challenged by unforeseen circumstances, organizational shifts, and misunderstandings about their intentions. They have to renegotiate old ground, for instance, when people move on and are replaced by others who replace them and need reinitiating. The art of systems convening is to sustain a consistent trajectory for a complex endeavor amidst all these changing and unpredictable circumstances.

Enabling long-term reconfiguration through short-term results. Going for the long haul and managing expectations are important. Sustaining fragile partnerships depends on short-term progress while making progress in cross-boundary partnerships requires time. Relationship building and creating a common language cannot be hurried as they are the foundation for learning together and collaborating. But while the work of reconfiguring the landscape is long term, people and institutions are impatient for results. Having brought people together across the landscape conveners then have to show that participating in the endeavor brings high value for the time they are investing. Conveners balance the long-term change necessary for their vision to come about with the short-term results that will keep people and organizations working with them.

> I was trying to make sure that everybody perceives at every stage that the benefits to them exceed the costs to them . . . It wasn't as if I could deliver everything, results, outcomes and so on, in one financial year, within one staff evaluation period, so you know, the bank is a little impatient . . . they say 'Show me results.' (JH)

With so many moving parts and while the ground is constantly shifting, conveners struggle to sustain their endeavor long enough and with enough coherence to make a difference. They hope that people will make progress in the domain while also committing to a new type of learning partnership that may challenge the status quo. Most conveners harbor a nagging suspicion that they must be crazy to try. But they plow on.

> A lot of it is just helping people see things in a different way. It's not that they were deliberately obstructive of change, but they may not have realized that change was a positive thing, so they just didn't make a positive effort to do it. (JH)

Convening work: reconfiguring identities

We have argued in Chapter 1 that people configure their identities by modulating relationships of accountability within a landscape. Reconfiguring the landscape entails identity work that will engender a sense of accountability to the new configuration. Reconfiguring identification is crucial because systems conveners rarely have formal authority over the people they need to involve in their endeavor.

Their efforts to reconfigure the landscape are very different from a top-down reorganization. The only way conveners can get people to join them is to allow them to make the endeavor their own – part of who they are and what they want to do. Conveners need to offer people new ways of seeing and experiencing themselves in the landscape. They have to go beyond simply inviting people into a project; they invite them to reconfigure their identity to become part of a reconfigured landscape.

To achieve this reconfiguration of identity, conveners work through the three 'modes of identification' introduced in Chapter 1 – imagination, engagement, and alignment.

The work of imagination: aspirational narratives

Conveners spark people's imagination and open up new aspirations for them.[5] What they propose is not just a vision. It is a new narrative about the landscape, its potential, and people's identities in it. Such an aspirational narrative invites a configuration of stakeholders to undertake something that no one thought possible. By articulating their vision into an aspirational narrative, systems conveners are in essence stoking people's imagination about the landscape and their role in it. The story they tell about the landscape reveals new potential latent in it.

This work of imagination, however, is difficult. Most conveners struggle to express their vision in ways that make sense to people. There are several reasons why this might be so:

- The vision they hold is often an incipient one, perhaps an intuition, an evolving hunch, rather than a well-formed vision of the final state.
- Whether a hunch or a well-formed vision, it may well be something that no one fully shares, especially in the beginning. Each participant or group holds only a small part of that vision.
- Conveners are well aware that to get traction their vision needs to be to a large extent co-created. Simply articulating it and waiting for people to live it does not work. Telling the narrative must be an invitation to a variety of stakeholders to share in its creation.

The challenge in sharing an aspirational narrative is to get people to identify with it, or at least a part of it, from their perspective. Conveners need to talk to a lot of people and rehearse their narrative with different audiences and in different settings. A growing part of our work in coaching and supporting systems conveners is to help them refine and rehearse the telling and retelling of the aspirational narrative – or versions of it – so that different stakeholders can recognize themselves and their own aspirations in it.

The work of engagement: boundaries as learning assets

Aspirational narratives can generate identification and inspire buy-in, but they are unlikely by themselves to bring about changes in practice. Conveners have to identify locations in the landscape where new forms of engagement across boundaries are likely to be productive. Then they need to facilitate meaningful encounters where people from relevant locations in the landscape can negotiate who they are to each other and what they can do together. This can be a challenge if people resist moving beyond familiar spaces that support traditional relationships and modes of engagement. Conveners need to entice them by designing boundary activities that stretch their understanding while also addressing key current concerns from their existing contexts.

Many systems conveners are practitioners in their field. Some are strategic thinkers. But they often do not have much experience designing for engagement and partnership. Yet it is key to making new partnerships work.

> People's understanding of the information isn't self-evident, so you have to facilitate and help people see old situations in new ways or see things for the first time. (JH)

Too often we have seen conveners view their design task as if interactive activities can simply be inserted into a traditional agenda; or they leave the design of the agenda for an administrator to create. But careful design of activities that enable productive cross-boundary encounters is

> I have been around and I've gone everywhere in the State honking this and it's like wow! And everyone thinks it's good in theory but then it kind of, well nothing happens! (NM)

an integral part of reconfiguring partnerships in the landscape. The most successful learning activities tend to engage people in doing something concrete relevant to stakeholders' practice and calling for collective engagement in negotiating significant issues:

- Focusing on practical issues of close relevance makes it more likely that challenges and mistakes are treated as opportunities for shared reflection and learning.
- Addressing concrete challenges where progress matters to all stakeholders makes it less likely that boundary interactions will degenerate into ideological school-of-thought fights.
- If people can engage their own practice in a boundary activity rather than simply listen to or visit someone else's practice, then participating in that activity is more likely to become transformative of their own practice.

Enabling such activities involves a variety of design elements:

- *Facilitating boundary crossing*, for example, involving certain people in brokering information across different stakeholder groups; creating or improving boundary objects, such as documents, that speak to people in different sectors; organizing visits to the practice of potential partners; devising projects that require people from different backgrounds to negotiate a common aim.
- *Designing for different types of learning spaces.* Different learning spaces support different kinds of interaction, from the formal to the informal, from structured to emergent,[6] from introspective to observing the practices of others.[7]
- *Using multiple ways to connect people.* Leveraging the affordances of technology and imaginative use of physical space to support multiple ways of connecting people across geographies, time, and differences.

Facilitating engagement in boundary encounters requires conveners to manage the balance of accountability and expressibility introduced in Chapter 1. Sustaining mutual engagement across boundaries entails new forms of account ability. However, expressibility is also an important factor, as relationships of power and accountability can easily marginalize or silence non-conforming views. Conveners pay attention to the expressibility of:

- **Voices**, especially the voices of people or groups who have not traditionally been involved. Reconfiguring the landscape through new forms of engagement can give a voice to groups or individuals who have previously not been heard, surfacing overt and subtle issues of power.
- **Differences**, whether they be differences in perspectives, goals, languages, or approaches. Paradoxically, working to make differences expressible is often a way to discover true mutual interest.
- **Power**, so the existence and nature of relationships of power among stakeholders become discussable. Again paradoxically, acknowledging power relations and reflecting on their effects, positive or negative, can be the best way to mitigate their potential harm to learning.

The idea of using boundaries as learning assets is to combine multiple voices and perspectives to create more complex forms of identification reflecting the landscape more broadly. Such meaningful engagement across boundaries is transformative:

- **Transformative of practice**. The differences, tensions, and conflicts that surface in boundary encounters have significant innovation potential when channeled into making progress on practical issues that matter to stakeholders.

- **Transformative of identity.** Engaged negotiation with a diversity of perspectives anchors knowledgeability in personal experience. Such direct and active encounters with other practices are conducive to reflection because they offer a chance to see oneself through other eyes. These encounters have the potential to yield both better knowledge of other practices and better understanding of one's own practice in its relation to the landscape.

The work of alignment: effectiveness at scale

Even successfully facilitated and personally inspiring boundary encounters will not sustain a broad and innovative endeavor aimed at transforming practice. Practice is embedded in complex systems operating at multiple levels of scale and changes in practice are rarely sustainable unless they involve realignment across the landscape.

To foster alignment, conveners propose aspirational narratives ambitious enough to transcend specific locations in the landscape. They challenge everyone rather than reflect the interests of specific stakeholders. Such alignment stretches the agendas of all stakeholders by including the perspective of a broader configuration, but it does not act as a replacement for these agendas. Participating in new configurations cannot detract people from pursuing their own agenda. This would be futile, unsustainable, and eventually counter-productive. People will not engage for long in an endeavor that takes them beyond their territory unless there is enough alignment with their own work.

The convener's push for alignment does not displace people's agendas; on the contrary it embraces these agendas to make them more ambitious, more connected, and in the end more likely to be effective.

This sounds grandiose, and it is; but in practice, it often takes the form of simply recognizing opportunities for enabling conversations, activities or projects that could achieve a valuable outcome for

> Having persuaded a number of stakeholders individually that this would be in their interest, I think you then have to identify what the impediments to getting into that improved state are and then you have to negotiate with a sufficient number of stakeholders for them to kind of make tradeoffs, compromises, put in a bit of effort they haven't done before, so that by contributing to this common exercise, they themselves are better off. (JH)

individuals while also contributing to the overall alignment of the endeavor and the weaving of new social relationships. These may be projects that people are already pursuing but that could achieve greater results when done in the context of cross-boundary collaboration in the landscape. Or they could be entirely new projects that serve and stretch the agendas of multiple stakeholders. Conveners often find themselves in a unique position to see such potential in disparate contexts. There is a method to it: recognizing the opportunity, connecting people around that opportunity, and providing just enough support to get the process going.

Effective conveners have a deep grasp of the overall endeavor and can see potential in smaller opportunities. They have a good sense of the landscape and know what matters. They understand enough about the perspectives of relevant stakeholders to create a relevant value proposition and are able to imagine the activities that would enable progress. This is how they work towards aligning people's participation with the overall vision.

Alignment is traditionally sought through top-down processes such as policies, program rollouts, and compliance audits. The alignment that conveners seek is of a different kind. It depends on reconfigured identities that embrace accountability in broader configurations. It is not based on compliance but on identification and knowledgeability:

- Identification with the endeavor and its multiple stakeholders.
- Knowledgeability about the points of articulation and disjunction in the landscape where alignment has to be sought and negotiated.

Conveners often have to spend time and resources convincing people in positions of power in organizations of the value of alignment through practice-based learning partnerships that focus on identification and knowledgeability. Indeed this type of mutual alignment takes time and effort. It appears more chaotic and less guaranteed than compliance with conventional top-down implementation. In the long run, however, it has the potential for more robust and sustained realization in practice.

Identification with the landscape

The work of imagination, engagement, and alignment produces a social learning process for reconfiguring identification – identification with a broader, more ambitious endeavor with other players in the landscape, and with effectiveness to be achieved across practices and at multiple levels of scale at once. The modes of identification are mutually reinforcing and all three are essential to the convener's endeavor:

- Not enough imagination – people do not see what is possible, where they are located in the broader picture, nor why they should take a risk with new configurations.
- Not enough engagement – the endeavor remains a dream or pro forma, other stakeholders remain distant abstractions, and the status quo is unlikely to be challenged.
- Not enough alignment – the endeavor does not achieve change at a scale sufficient to make a real difference in practice.

Indeed, conveners seek to increase the knowledgeability of people in the landscape with the idea that this has got to lead to new synergies and capabilities.

Often couched in terms like 'sharing knowledge,' it is really a process of becoming more knowledgeable about other people's practices which may have some bearing on one's own. This opens up new avenues for making progress in the field. Conveners have an aspirational narrative that may represent their vision, but they do not have a fixed agenda which they attempt to roll out. By exposing people to new views and experiences of the landscape, by opening up their imagination to what's possible, and by forging new relationships, they attempt to produce new forms of knowledgeability and let this new knowledgeability shape what people do. They make people more knowledgeable about the landscape so their reconfigured identities lead to new behaviors. Over time the convener's endeavor increasingly makes sense to people who are able to appropriate this vision for themselves. The resulting increase in knowledgeability provides a foundation for new forms of participation oriented to the landscape.

Being a convener: the reconfiguring spirit

The work of systems convening is not for the faint of heart; but it is not for the reckless or the high-handed either. It calls for an unusual mix of boldness and humility, calculation and risk. Indeed, it is the strength and the frailty of the work of conveners that they are themselves part of the landscape. They do not occupy a privileged position outside of it; they toil within it. They are not puppeteers; they are travelers. Their work as convener is part of their own learning journey through the very landscape they are trying to reconfigure. In this journey, the reconfiguring of their own identity inspires and informs their attempt to reconfigure the landscape.

Systems convening is intensely personal work. It is therefore fitting to end this chapter with some observations about the person of the convener. While conveners come in all shapes and sizes, operate at different levels of scale, and have different relationships to the landscape, we have noted some interesting patterns. Reflecting the tensions inherent in their work, the life of conveners is an exercise in paradoxes. It takes someone with an unusual mix of characteristics and poise to tread these paradoxes.

On a personal mission

Conveners are driven by a very personal sense of mission. They feel a commitment to long-term, sustainable results that go beyond narrow individual aspirations.

This personal sense of mission is essential. It is what makes them convincing and allows them to use their own journey as a source of inspiration for creating aspirational narratives. It is also what sustains

> This is a really corny thing: I want to make a difference. So I as an individual accountant just doing my individual job wouldn't change the world for the better, but if I want to help contribute to positive change, I need to leverage the involvement of others . . . (JH)

them through uncertainty, lack of recognition, outright opposition, and even doubt about themselves.

> . . . certainly I doubt my own skills but I don't doubt this vision. (NM)

Successful conveners are driven by a personal mission, but they are able to invite others into this mission in such a way that the ownership of the mission is shared. They do not let their overriding sense of mission translate into an urge to control.

They let others construct the narrative with them. While they open spaces for learning and instigate change they also invite others to shape the agenda and develop solutions.

> There's some ownership there, it's not top-down which I think has been really important, and they see the benefit of participating. That here they have access to this wealth of information and they can also be included . . . so that they're a player in this and contributing . . . (NM)

We have not yet met a convener who micro-manages. They find the right people to take leadership and work with them or take a back seat on the implementation.

They welcome and appreciate others' enthusiasm for the endeavor and respect the integrity of their commitment. There is, however, a vulnerability for conveners in this openness to others taking leadership.

> We're really trying to change the way we do business and education in Iowa and we have a plan, but everyone is doing it independently and that's like – we will never get it done in our State if we take that approach. (NM)

They can find it difficult to assess their contribution, guide them, or rein them in. Their desire to engage others can make them susceptible to prolonged confidence or reliance in the wrong person.

Promoting others' leadership also requires a delicate balance. Strategically working behind the scenes, where the more effective they are the less visible they will be, conveners also need to demonstrate the work that they do. There is a tension in giving credit for results to those who join and take leadership in the endeavor as they risk prematurely losing the resources for their own work.

Passionate and strategic

> It is difficult to describe what 'goes on behind' what people see without feeling as though 'you are taking credit' by telling how hard *you* worked. Conveners must express these tasks and overcome feeling boastful or 'martyr like.' (Joanne Cashman, see Chapter 9)

Driven by their passion, conveners are idealistic and given to impatience. There is a pioneering spirit in most conveners we meet.[8]

They are social innovators paving the way for solving complex problems, driven by a certainty that much can be achieved if they can just bring the right combination of people to the table.

They are spearheading a vision that transcends traditional boundaries, organizational divisions, and institutional narrow-mindedness. They are ambitious and bold and tend not to let concerns about details get in the way.

> Certainly if there was support and funding and everybody was saying, yes let's do this, but truly, it's about being bold. Let's go after it, we have to! It's just time . . . (NM)

And yet they have to combine this passion and enthusiasm for what they believe is possible with the pragmatism necessary to make it happen. They manage a tension between the personal passion and charisma it takes to convince people to become involved on the one hand, and careful calculations on the other hand – to seed the right ideas, create useful connections, initiate appropriate activities and projects, and justify to organizational sponsors the resources it takes to make progress. They are dreamers but they are also schemers, with a solid dose of strategic thinking and tactical acuity.

Mavericks at the edge in their own organization

Conveners themselves are usually affiliated with an institution in the landscape; but the complex, dynamic, and personal work of systems convening is inherently at odds with the more rigid structures of the organizations whose support and sponsorship conveners have to seek. As a result, conveners tend to play at the edge of what is permissible in their (and others') organizations.

As organizational mavericks stretching the bounds of what is possible conveners are easily misunderstood, unrecognized, or undervalued. Skeptics are often waiting in the wings for small failures.

Conveners can burn out or get moved on by their organizations before they can see through their long-term vision. And while they channel their convening energy through an organization they believe in, they are often dismayed by the organizational procedures they will have to go through to make things happen: hierarchies to be accountable to, policies to

> Had I known that this position or this initiative were going to go forward, I would have been doing things in December to get ready for all of these next steps. Instead I've had to go around . . . in limbo – and then just had to say: wait, we don't know . . . (NM)

comply with, procedures to follow, and support that depends on producing specific types of data to demonstrate the value of what is happening. Conveners take risks as they pursue their vision while navigating these expectations. These risks leave them vulnerable to political winds or changes in leadership. A lot of convening work is not easily visible to hierarchies. Focusing on long-term effects finds little resonance. The job of conveners is easily threatened by changing economic circumstances and organizational restructuring. Often they cannot be certain that their job is secure enough to see the project through or to plan beyond the next step. Conveners may be pragmatic, aware of different interests in the landscape, and politically astute; but their endeavor is such that these

> One of the dimensions I've neglected is my safety net. I think that's very important, very significant. (JH)

qualities in the service of their vision do not always save them from rather precarious positions in their own organization.

Mavericks in their organizations, conveners can feel like lone rangers. Often the only person who fully grasps the potential that exists across boundaries conveners can tread a rather lonely path. Behind the cheerful face and sanguine disposition is someone who craves companionship and understanding. Yet so accustomed are they to being robust loners in the landscape that they rarely seek out other conveners in neighboring landscapes to ask for help or advice. A supportive network is important, however, as the kinds of challenges conveners face call for attention to personal support and self-care.

Legitimacy and knowledgeability: at home, everywhere, and nowhere

As an invitation, convening requires legitimacy, but legitimacy is problematic across boundaries.

> . . . you need a certain technical and related standing to be credible; I mean people have to allow you into the room. (JH)

Whatever source of legitimacy gives them an entry point into the landscape – reputation, technical competence, organizational support, access to funding – they work hard not to be perceived as colonizers. They strive to make participation in a landscape-oriented endeavor a contribution to local practice rather than a distracting additional task. Their legitimacy is deep enough to engender respect and yet broad enough to transcend boundaries and invite widespread engagement.

Systems conveners are both at home and misfits in most locations of the landscape, with no obvious location for their identity. They may not be competent in any one thing, but have enough of a history in the landscape to have a cross-boundary perspective. They are knowledgeable about the shape of the landscape and the ways various practices articulate.

They appreciate different forms of competence enough to leverage them. This gives them a fine-tuned sensibility to good ideas. It allows them to opportunistically pick up potentially relevant suggestions from different parts of the landscape and weave them into an overall strategy. Being knowledgeable rather than competent can make them vulnerable to inappropriate suggestions.

> Having this vantage point of having been in this system a while and been in several different roles and then being able to kind of look at it from a bird's eye view has just been really very, very valuable for me. (NM)

Their sensitivity to new ideas and hunger for cross-boundary innovations can push them to leap on proposals based on superficial understanding, immune to corrections that represent a local understanding.

And yet it is precisely this ability to grasp the possible beyond local certainties that makes them such an important contributor.

Upbeat and persistent

Given the long-term nature of their commitment and the likelihood of temporary setbacks, perhaps the key characteristic of successful conveners is persistence.

Something keeps them going in spite of many obstacles. Conveners meet with plenty of resistance and go through times when giving up seems like the more reasonable option. Even though they come to embody the endeavor and invest their personal social capital in it, they take on the resistance rather stoically.

> You just kind of take it on the chin … with a confidence in the long-term rightness of what you're doing and just weather the storm … (JH)

> Where I get a bloody nose is getting those … sponsors to see what we're doing and to see the value that it's adding to our State. (NM)

Yet they embrace unexpected obstacles and resistance with a sort of dogged positivism that drives the process. They remain upbeat as they keep the project alive and moving even when things are not going well.

They tend to be optimistic, even over-optimistic, and their positive spin often fuels the endeavor, especially in the early stages. Their optimism extends to people as well as goals and setbacks: conveners tend to be generous in their attribution of intentions, their respect, and their compliments, especially to key players on whom the project depends.

> If you want to get people engaged and enthused and so on, you have to be optimistic, you have to believe that positive things can happen. You know, is the glass half full, is it half empty? (JH)

> I'm the chief enthusiast so if I can pick myself up today and get up there and give the great cheer, I think that's been very helpful for people. (NM)

However necessary for spearheading a difficult initiative, being upbeat and persistent exacts a price. It can lead conveners to underestimate how long it takes to transform practices and identities, address boundary differences, or change organizational cultures. Spending a lot of time and effort fighting the reality of the landscape in the name of a legitimate cause can make the reality more difficult to see. And the need to be upbeat all the time can make it seem as though being critical or self-critical is a betrayal. While essential to overcoming obstacles and inspiring others to keep going, dogged positivism exists in tension with the need for critical reflection and realistic assessment.

> I suppose one can sometimes get a little bit over enthused about the constant push forward without always looking back to make sure that everything is in place. (JH)

A discipline of systems convening: leadership for the twenty-first century

Systems conveners fulfill a critical function in landscapes of practice. If we have made it sound like an impossible job, it's because it is. Working with a number of people who have taken it on, we have developed a kind of puzzled reverence for conveners, whether they succeed or fail. Taking on an impossible job may well be the only way to push the boundaries of what is possible in a complex landscape of practice.

Describing the challenges, work, and characteristics of systems conveners is a step toward recognizing their role and providing an environment conducive to their success. Conveners themselves need to see that their situation is not unique; many others face the same struggles. The people they convene need to appreciate the work of those who prod them to move beyond their comfort zones. And organizations need to understand what conveners do and the value they bring so they can provide needed support – or at least avoid creating obstacles.

We see systems conveners as pioneers of a new type of leadership. They fulfill a critical need in the twenty-first century. Issues that brought people together in the past tended to be local and geographically based. They were mostly structured along organizational, disciplinary, or sectoral interests. Today, complex problems require cross-disciplinary thinking, local problems call for regional or global responses, and societal issues require cross-sector partnerships. At the same time markets, business processes, government services, and education are moving towards more networked approaches. Web and mobile technologies are transforming the possibilities for connecting and supporting new types of peer-to-peer interactions. These trends require us to be more reflexive about leadership in complex landscapes; they call for processes and approaches that are still being invented. Our work with some pioneers of this art has started our inquiry into an emerging discipline of systems convening.

The discipline is in its infancy. We need stories of systems conveners at different levels of scale, not just high-level conveners with enough organizational visibility to be easily recognized. There seem to be different types of systems conveners – from those who sponsor the endeavor, to those who drive it, to those who implement it. On a practical level are questions about tools and practices. What tools would help them create visual maps of the landscape to articulate its potential to different stakeholders? What questions and activities are likely to engage people across boundaries? What understanding of learning would help them articulate the new configuration of partnerships in a compelling way? What approaches would enable them to capture and scale up learning in a landscape? On a strategic level, we need to better understand the power structures that support the work of conveners, or get in their way. We also need methods for assessing and articulating their impact on the landscape. Pursuing these and many other questions will be necessary to build the discipline of systems convening so it can contribute to some of the leadership challenges we face today.

Notes

1. Craig and Patricia Neal (2011) write about the 'art of convening' where they are concerned with how a facilitator gathers and holds people in a close and generative space that leads to effective or authentic engagement between individuals. The convener is someone who is concerned with minute-by-minute and day-by-day moments of genuine and transformative conversations that lead to positive outcomes. Kate Pugh (2011), a knowledge management consultant and author of *Knowledge Jam*, talks of conveners as 'Collaboration Glue.' The Collaborative Leaders Network of Hawaii identifies conveners as a vital part of their strategy for bringing diverse groups of people together to solve the state's problems. For this network a convener is 'an individual or group responsible for bringing people together to address an issue, problem, or opportunity . . . usually . . . from multiple sectors for a multi-meeting process, typically on complex issues . . . Conveners use their influence and authority to collaborate' (The Collaborative Leaders Network, n.d.).
2. Melinda Gates of the Gates Foundation describes the Foundation as a convener of people and projects (*The Economist*, 2006). The former senior partner of strategy and innovation at the World Bank refers to the bank as 'Convener first, lender second' (Whittle, 2011). The Clinton Global Initiative proposes to use 'convening power' as a way to achieve their mission: to inspire, connect, and empower a community of global leaders to forge solutions to the world's most pressing challenges (http://www.clintonglobalinitiative.org/aboutus/).
3. In a *Time Magazine* article (2011), Hillary Clinton talks about this as smart power, which is the forming of coalitions and the use of new media to foster development aid and public–private collaboration (p. 18). She used her smart power as U.S. Secretary of State to broker conversations between different government heads, non-governmental organizations, women's groups and other interest groups. Her style of brokering coalitions and paying attention to the affordances and transparency of new technology marks a shift in traditional methods of diplomacy that used military or economic power to leverage control.
4. In this chapter, when we use the term convener for simplification, we are referring to 'systems convener.'
5. This idea is related in part to the idea of 'legitimating accounts' proposed by Creed et al. (2002) to describe how social activists interpret and adapt ideas to local logics and settings to provide common meanings and identities that mobilize local participation.
6. Roy Williams, Jenny Mackness, and Simone Guntau (2012) have developed a tool called 'footprints of emergence' for reflecting on a learning environment on a scale between prescribed and emergent.
7. In her dissertation, Sue Smith has identified four different types of learning spaces in her work as a convener: the peer-to-peer space for mutual learning, the social space for building relationship, the reflective space, and the peripheral space through which learning extends to other contexts (Smith, 2011).
8. This is related to the concept of 'institutional entrepreneurs' Institution Theory. Fligstein (2001), for example, proposes that these entrepreneurs are skilled strategic actors who find ways to get disparate groups to cooperate by providing common meanings and identities. The vision of a systems convener is to change the learning and problem-solving capability of a system over the long term by opening new spaces and making new connections. Their transformation of a system is usually beyond any institutional context.

References

Creed, W. E. D., Scully, M. A., & Austin, J. R. (2002). Clothes make the person? The tailoring of legitimating accounts and the social construction of identity. *Organization Science*, 13(5): 475–496.

The Collaborative Leaders Network (n.d.). http://collaborativeleadersnetwork.org. Accessed December 8, 2013.

The Economist (2006). The new powers in giving. http://www.economist.com/node/7112702. Accessed December 8, 2013.

Fligstein, N. (2001). Social skill and the theory of fields. *Sociological Theory*, 19(2): 105–125.

Neal, C. and Neal, P. 2011. *The Art of Convening: Authentic Engagement in Meetings, Gatherings, and Conversations.* San Francisco, CA: Berrett-Kohler Publishers.

Pugh, K. 2011. *Sharing Hidden Know-How: How Managers Solve Thorny Problems With the Knowledge Jam.* New York: John Wiley & Sons, Incorporated.

Smith, S. (2011). *SME leaders' learning in networked learning: An Actor-network theory and Communities of Practice theory informed analysis.* Unpublished dissertation, University of Lancaster, UK.

Time Magazine (2011). Hillary Clinton & the rise of smart power. November 7, 2011, vol. 178 no. 18.

Whittle, D. (2011). The World Bank as convener first, lender second? In *The Huffington Post*, July 27, 2011. http://www.huffingtonpost.com/dennis-whittle/the-world-bank-as-convene_b_910382.html? Accessed December 8, 2013.

Williams, R., Mackness, J., & Gumtau, S. (2012). Footprints of emergence. *International Review of Research in Open and Distance Learning*, 13, 4. http://www.irrodl.org/index.php/irrodl/article/view/1267. Accessed December 8, 2013.

Chapter 7

Habiforum

Convening stakeholders to reinvent spatial planning

Marc Coenders, Robert Bood,
Beverly Wenger-Trayner and
Etienne Wenger-Trayner

Habiforum is the name of a project initiated by the Dutch government to facilitate the transition from traditional top-down spatial planning, or development of plans for land-use, to a new inclusive paradigm involving all stakeholders in a broader process of area development. The practices that needed to be cultivated under this new paradigm were not known when the project began. The hope was that the right practices would emerge if the project took up the following series of actions: explicitly convert the spatial planning agenda to this new paradigm, convene stakeholders and professionals from different fields, and help them work together more deliberately to develop new approaches and methodologies.

This chapter starts by giving a picture of the challenge of traditional approaches to spatial planning and then describes how Habiforum has convened stakeholders from different fields in ways that engage them in a broader and more involved process of area development. A reflection on the different projects highlights some of the convening practices that contributed to its successes as does a reflection on the role of the 'master' convener in the Habiforum project.

Fragmentation in a complex landscape of practice

In a small country with a large population like the Netherlands, space is a scarce resource. Spatial planning is a complex process that involves a wide range of stakeholders with diverse and often conflicting practices and interests, and with varying ability to influence the results. This landscape of practice includes government agencies from national to local, architects, developers, landowners, not-for-profit organizations, as well as local communities, businesses, and scientists. Traditionally, these actors have maintained clear boundaries to keep the process simple and to avoid conflicts of interest. Professionals from different disciplines largely work in isolation. There is little interaction among different government levels, policy-making and project work, public and private organizations, and competing firms. Scientists and practitioners live in different worlds.

Traditional spatial planning has too often led to the alienation of communities and other stakeholders affected by the planning process. The expectations of all involved are diverse and, at first glance, irreconcilable. The highest government level involved, often a federal or regional agency, by and large dominates the process. The master plans and generic directives prescribed by federal or regional governments often fall short of meeting the requirements of specific situations and local contexts. The dynamics of environmental circumstances, local histories, and diverse stakeholders do not comfortably align with broader financial, industrial, or economic policy objectives and priorities. As a result plans and proposals developed on the drawing tables of federal and regional governments tend to fall short of meeting the needs and expectations of local stakeholders.

Typical Habiforum project 1: The Overdiepse Polder[1]

Located in a southeastern province of the Netherlands, the Overdiepse Polder was designated by the federal government as a buffer area to temporarily store excess water when rivers reached high levels. It was part of a nation-wide project called 'Room for the river', but it did not follow the traditional approach of a federal agency leading the design and planning of the 'best solution'. Such top-down solutions would easily conflict with the interests of the farmers who lived and worked in the reclaimed marshland of the polder. To prevent a potential stalemate – the government wanting to displace farmers to create a spillway and farmers not wanting to leave – ample space was given to experiment with novel solutions that would meet the seemingly intractable interests of all stakeholders. Facilitators from the Habiforum community helped the different stakeholders through a process of generating ideas by engaging at the boundaries between formal organizations and informal networks, the interests of water storage and agriculture, and the development and implementation of policies. Although the regional government was formally appointed as the project leader, local residents and other stakeholders took an active leadership role in the process. This unusual approach resulted in a remarkable solution. The Overdiepse Polder would become a spillway but the government would also construct a number of mounds along the southern edge that could withstand high water levels. New farms could be built on these mounds – or terps – and most farmers would be able to stay.

On paper, the planning process is neatly arranged along a linear path from the exploration of a situation, to a proposal to proceed, to the development of a spatial plan, and to implementation and maintenance. The plan specifies objectives to be reached in a certain time-frame. In practice, the process is more problematic. Challenges typically consist of an intricate web of interconnected problems, some technical, others economic or social. The precise outcomes are not certain. Stakes are high and stakeholders often disagree on the problem and its solution. Some seek change while others keep pushing familiar, standardized solutions that keep the status quo. The fragmented nature of spatial planning encourages people to defend the positions represented by the group they feel most accountable to. Stakeholders are more interested in their stake in the negotiation than in the overall quality of the final design. New ideas and concepts are often marginalized because they only complicate an already tough negotiation process. As a result many of these problems can have long histories that sometimes last for decades. And even when solutions are reached, they are often suboptimal compromises that lack aesthetic and innovative integrity.

By contrast, the best solutions to complex spatial planning challenges are tailor-made and developed locally with all stakeholders working closely together. This approach to planning is less about the arbitration of competing views than one of partnering in and facilitating development. It requires careful consideration of how to create a process where constructive conversations between stakeholders can happen. The approach that fulfils this requirement is referred to as 'area development'. The case of the 'Overdiepse Polder' illustrates the strength of this approach.

Convening as an approach to innovation

The approach taken in the Overdiepse Polder has its history in a long-running project. In the late 1990s, a small team at the Dutch Ministry of Transport, Public Works and Water Management launched the idea of a knowledge-creation programme solely focused on developing innovative approaches to spatial planning. They knew that any programme that took up this challenge would need to come from outside the Ministry, which had dominated the field for so long. Only an independent organization would be able to break the perception of inequality between the Minister and other public and private parties involved, and challenge entrenched ways so they could explore new approaches. Since its inception in 1999, what became known as Habiforum operated as an independent entity. Soon after seconding a member of his staff from the Ministry to Habiforum, Ab van Luin, a self-professed 'coalition builder',[2] decided to join the project himself as deputy director. Ab took up responsibility for Habiforum's practice programme, which complemented the academic programme and aimed to create new professional practices in the field of spatial planning.

The initial idea was to create a centre of excellence that would bring together selected experts to develop a new approach. When that failed to materialize, Ab rewrote the proposal to focus instead on an 'expertise network', with only a small staff supporting a large network of partners and professionals. His vision was that they would be able to use the expertise spread across the landscape of practice rather than relying on a single centre acting as the source of knowledge. Forming a network was an open invitation to professionals and organizations from all branches of spatial planning to work together in creating new knowledge and practices. Ab became a systems convener.

In his attempt to reconfigure the landscape, Ab's first action was to invite a range of professionals from different streams in spatial planning as well as from the field of organizational learning to submit proposals for creating new practices together. The condition was that each proposal had to be submitted by a consortium of different partners. To stimulate the formation of new consortia he organized a series of meetings to bring a diversity of people and organizations together. His intention had been to finance one or two of the best proposals, but this changed after a conversation with one of the applicants. The applicant, an internationally renowned landscape architect, pointed to the high quality of the proposals and asked why Habiforum did not simply take them all. In response to that idea Ab put together a co-financing model in which Habiforum financed up to half of a proposal and the applicants the rest. A prerequisite for receiving matching funds was a commitment to share all learning from the projects openly, in gatherings with others, in booklets, and on the internet.[3] This model certainly contributed to the commitment of organizations to participate actively in Habiforum's network and to share their knowledge and experience.

Typical Habiforum project 2: Renewal of rural areas

Habiforum hosted a series of projects concerned with developing a customized approach to the renewal of rural areas. The projects were attempts to restore quality of life and vitality in areas that had complicated, area-specific problems. The kinds of problems include an exodus of farmers, an increase in large-scale farming concepts ill-suited to the land, shrinking areas, and migration of residents between regions. Each project required tailored solutions and policies as well as new relations with government agencies. Yet the projects also shared fundamental questions about the respective roles of regional and local governments, residents, and private companies. The traditionally dominant role of government had often left the entrepreneurial potential and social capital of both residents and companies largely untapped. Each project needed to tread a delicate path toward the goal of engaging the experience, networks, expertise, and ideas of all stakeholders. A renowned advisor in the field leveraged the shared context of Habiforum to bring these pioneers together in a community of practice to make progress on these fundamental challenges in area development. Over a period of two years, the community of practice worked on five concrete projects. Members included policy makers, entrepreneurs, and consultants, who were each experimenting with new ways of working in their respective domains. By sharing stories, ideas, and experiences across projects and professions, they developed innovative practices to increase the voice and responsibility of residents in the development of the rural area where they lived. Their efforts led to new kinds of public–private cooperation and strengthened the social capital of areas where projects were run.

Around that time, Ab came across the concept of communities of practice in a magazine. After exploring the concept further, Ab realized that the team's intuition 'suddenly had gotten a name'. He saw this approach as a way for all kinds of people working in the domain of spatial planning to come together across professions, hierarchies, and formal organizations. They could bring diverse perspectives to bear in forging new knowledge and practices to address the most difficult challenges in the field.

We got to work with communities of practice in 2000 with only that basic awareness and an attitude that experience is always the best teacher. Just meeting does not lead to anything new. Sharing knowledge is not enough. The key is to create knowledge. To do so requires both universities that do basic research and a range of professionals who carry out the work in practice. I saw an opportunity for both to work together in communities of practice.

Through the idea of communities of practice, new configurations of people and organizations were formed around a range of topics like business parks, water and space, regional nodes, city regeneration, and rural areas renewal (see project 2). Each community worked in partnership to explore concrete cases that would help them develop better solutions. Although networking and convening new cross-boundary communities across the landscape was central to Habiforum, not all attempts at crossing boundaries were successful. At the core of the vision of Habiforum was the cross-fertilization between research and practice. By actively sharing their knowledge, researchers and practitioners would enrich their respective work and out of this synergy produce new approaches. This initial aspiration was not achieved, however: although research and practice development were linked at the project level, the boundary between them proved impermeable. For administrative reasons research and practice were organized as independent programmes with separate budgets and proposal submissions. A professor with a very high reputation in the field headed the research programme and coordinated it from his university. Ab, who was the director of the practice programme, worked from Habiforum's office. They organized their programmes in fundamentally different ways. In contrast to Ab's approach of including different voices from across the landscape in an exploratory way, the scientific director wanted specific topics to be rigorously researched with specific outcomes before being applied in the programme.

The two perspectives on the nature of knowledge, its creation, and application only grew further apart as the practitioner programme developed and the difference in outlooks between practitioners and researchers became clearer. Practitioners consider research insights as one of many sources to inform their practice. Researchers tend to adopt the subsumption perspective described in Chapter 1. In their eyes the outputs of research are to subsume the perspectives of practitioners: they presume that once research has created and articulated new insights, practitioners will simply apply this knowledge in their practice.

Despite Ab's optimism, the difference turned out to be irreconcilable. The two directors recognized their differences and met to discuss them, but were unable to bridge their views and link the two programmes. After a few years Ab pragmatically reduced his efforts to bridge the gap and focused instead on the practice programme. Eventually, researchers and practitioners formed two largely independent, and independently successful, networks. The research programme generated over 1,000 scientific articles and dozens of dissertations. The practice programme connected thousands of practitioners in the field, who worked together in hundreds of projects and created a wide range of new practices and spatial solutions. Although both programmes were successful in their own terms, the divide between them proved too difficult and only incidentally did the two benefit from being part of the same initiative.

Even with limited interest from his academic counterpart, Ab continued to focus the practice programme on convening as an approach to innovation. The communities-of-practice model allowed stakeholders to convene around specific topics, projects, and cases in urban and rural planning. By opening up new spaces between practices, organizations, and project phases the approach substantially increased the room for experimentation. Rather than passing through a series of prescribed steps, participants were able to move back and forth seamlessly between different phases of the development process. The model offered a stimulating context to experiment with a diverse range of approaches where people developed a sense of accountability to new perspectives and where they could openly share insights and outcomes to make sense of their experiences across cases. The 'Gardens for the creative economy' project illustrates this mix of experimentation and shared reflection across project phases (see project 3).

Typical Habiforum project 3: Gardens for the creative economy

A third example was a series of 'experimental gardens' for the creative economy. Stimulating local creative economies requires activities in domains like design, media, communication, education, and the arts crucial for new entrepreneurial ideas. Yet these 'cultural entrepreneurs' often lack an environment that provides both space and a community of like-minded people. At the same time old factory buildings are decaying right in the centre of many cities. An experienced consultant and former alderman of the city of Amsterdam acted as a convener and facilitator for a group of local initiatives from eight Dutch cities to explore how to restore old factory buildings into dedicated spaces for housing local creative economies. The group's goal was to shift from the dominant discourse of redevelopment into offices and condominiums toward a discourse highlighting the value of cultural activities and local entrepreneurship. They started to learn together by organizing workshops in which each initiative was explored by the group and, if deemed necessary, specific experts. The shared purpose was to breathe new life into those old factory buildings and find support and capital from local governments, entrepreneurs, and project developers. In all participating cities old factories have been turned into creative centres that are home to designers and artists of all kinds, theatre groups, social entrepreneurs, and small shops. Initiatives often conflicted with the agenda of local politicians who preferred a blueprint approach and master plans instead of the emerging approach advocated in the project. The network has enriched and accelerated these local initiatives, many of which would otherwise not have been realized at all.

Coming right after publication of the report *The Netherlands is full*, Habiforum's approach to the use of limited space was timely. Such an offer to all stakeholders to participate in shaping the domain had never come from the Ministry. This was certainly the case for private parties like engineering companies and project developers who had always been approached suspiciously. The idea of communities in which people share their respective practices, interact, and create new knowledge was novel in the field of spatial planning and even the Netherlands at large. Instead of 'scientific knowledge' that had to be translated into practice, it introduced a new perspective on knowledge creation as a living process involving multiple perspectives. Essentially for the first time practitioners were offered the opportunity to join in the conversation as equal partners at an early stage with a minimum of formal restrictions.

Habiforum soon attracted practitioners from all over the field of spatial planning for whom the work now resonated with their own goals. Their interest went far beyond Habiforum's expectations. From the start Ab was amazed by their willingness to invest time and effort in projects that were often quite open ended. They welcomed what they considered a rare opportunity to develop new ways of working in close cooperation with other stakeholders beyond the often-strict boundaries of their organizations. Contributing to the design of new solutions proved to be a lot more stimulating than having to work with predetermined formats largely dictated by government agencies. Over the years, hundreds of professionals initiated projects to convene practitioners from different backgrounds, disciplines, and practices to learn together. These projects ranged from focused efforts consisting of a small number of reflection sessions to extensive programmes spread out over several years. Many displayed a spirit of pioneering and exploring new grounds. The new paradigm of 'area development' as well as many of the tools and methods introduced and developed by Habiforum have become common in the field of spatial planning. While Habiforum formally ended in 2009, the rich trove of experiments, practices, insights, and experiences it produced are still very much alive. The website that covers all the methods and insights is still widely visited today.

Key convening practices

Given the focus on customized solutions and the diversity of cases, approaches, and personalities involved in projects over the years, it is hard to describe the Habiforum approach in general. Systems convening does not follow clear step-by-step plans that can easily be copied by others. Various conveners in Habiforum have their own styles and ways of forging learning partnerships and their art includes tacit skills and intuitions that even they cannot explain fully. Yet, one can discern several key convening practices common across the various projects.

Inviting an 'enterprising group' of stakeholders

The first key practice is that of ensuring that the right configuration of people is invited, even if they have never been in the same conversation before.

Conveners need to be very knowledgeable about the problem situation to appreciate both the technical challenges and the diversity of actors, ambitions, and interests. They excel in connecting the personal drive of people and ensure that all key stakeholders are included – whether they have a stake in the challenge or can contribute to resolving it. If required, conveners also invite outside experts who can offer their views on the situation and enrich proposed ideas. The strength of the conveners' invitation comes from their reputation in the field and the vivid way they can summarize the essence of the problem situation in a few intriguing questions or phrases that communicate both urgency and inspiration. In most cases they stand right in the middle of the landscape rather than outside of it. Opening up opportunities to contribute to the setting of the goal and approach turns out to be crucial. One of the early projects failed from the start when invited stakeholders were confronted with a complete design/ solution created by an architect, which meant that there was only a marginal role left for them to fulfil.

It is crucial to have the 'whole system' present, but the point is not merely to get everybody in the room, have them talk shop, and avoid chaos. Conveners aim for an 'enterprising group' of people whose circumstances and priorities enable them to take risks and responsibility in dealing with the problem in new ways. A good example is the drive of the citizen group in the case of the old railway workshop (see project 4). Conveners also make clear from the start that coming only to 'take' is not acceptable and that bringing something to the table is a condition for joining. Habiforum facilitators will not hesitate to look for substitutes to replace individuals whose other commitments mean they cannot participate actively in the enterprising spirit of the group.

Typical Habiforum project 4: The old railway workshop

Another spatial challenge was to find a new purpose for an old carriage-repair depot belonging to the Dutch National Railways. Stuck between a residential district and the city centre, the collection of buildings had turned into a twilight zone only a few years after it had become obsolete. But when demolition became imminent, a small group of local residents recognized the potential beauty of this unique industrial inheritance. At the start of the project, the owner of the buildings and grounds did not see their potential and the local government had nothing to say about the area. Local residents lacked a formal position, but they managed to put the project on top of the local political agenda. While they were able to get official status for the buildings as a monument, real progress only came when a professional facilitator became involved to help the group take their initiative to the next level. They invited other stakeholders, including the local government, a range of not-for-profit organizations, entrepreneurs, and the Dutch National Railways to a meeting. Together they started to imagine new uses for the old depot and the surrounding areas, and the noncommittal attitude of stakeholders morphed into strong personal relations and active involvement. All acknowledged that the development of the area was both too important and too complex to leave to a single party. The collective learning that took place from the interactions of these different perspectives led to the discovery of all kinds of new purposes for the depot. Many buildings have been restored and put into new use, often by a company or organization working in the cultural or artistic domain. The terrain now includes a theatre for festivities and conferences as well as office buildings hosting architects, designers, and event organizers. A master plan for the entire area describes how it will be developed further in the coming years. Due to its proximity to the station, the area is now praised for its regional and even national potential.

Such enterprising groups do not gather merely to pursue their individual interests or negotiate compromises. These professionals from different communities must be ready to interweave their practices, perspectives, and competencies to explore possibilities and take action as a group. This entails a responsibility to engage seriously across boundaries without knowing future outcomes beforehand and to build on each other's practices to develop new practices as a group. It requires a sense of accountability to a new configuration of actors involved in (re-)thinking the solution.

Building trust and openness by making power discussable

The difficult situations typical of Habiforum projects require exploring, probing, experimenting, and learning with an open attitude. Yet, stakeholders are likely to have known of each other for years; they often find themselves stuck in a deadlock. A key role of conveners is to break such deadlocks by creating a new, open atmosphere that allows stakeholders to interact in a constructive way. The 'political' nature of this work has both external and internal dimensions.

Externally, conveners strive simultaneously to buffer the new initiative from mainstream politics while trying at the same time to get ample political support for it. In the case of the Overdiepse Polder 'power' was seized by seeking publicity or calling upon a former minister. The case of the old railway workshop shows how personal this process can become (see project 4). A powerful local politician, who was a strong supporter of the project, was frequently mobilized to give new impetus to the process. Indeed Ab notes the importance of finding a politician who is personally moved to make something happen politically. This work is ongoing as the political scenario evolves and people move in and out of positions of power.

Internally, facilitators strive to create 'power-full' learning spaces, in which key actors and stakeholders can freely confront their various interests, ambitions, conflicts, and potential alignment. For instance, in the 'creative economy' project (see project 3), the interests of all stakeholders were articulated and put openly on the table. The Habiforum facilitators make an important distinction between 'power-full' spaces and 'power-free' ones. An atmosphere of trust is often associated with the idea of a more comfortable power-free space. A power-free space may enable faster progress during the early stages but cause the project to lose steam when ideas have to be put into practice. In a 'power-full' space, trust develops from the expressibility of what is going on: articulating issues of power and making them discussable. These issues are recognized as an inherent aspect of boundary engagement. Discussing them openly provides an opportunity for stakeholders to get to know each other at a personal level. Formal power has to be discussable in the process of reaching and mobilizing personal drives and energy underneath. Once people engage with each other on a personal level, they find it easier to see boundaries as institutional artefacts they need to deal with together. This can only happen when the process is open ended, when learning can freely drive that process, and when the outcome is not pre-determined. Solutions can then be found, which were 'unreachable' before.

Creating commitment by mobilizing around ambitious goals

A fundamental principle of the new paradigm of area development is to deliberately strive for planning solutions of the highest overall quality rather than a compromise that satisfies the lowest common denominator. Such solutions strive to enhance the area without losing existing characteristics that are valued. As it turns out this principle is also a key convening practice: people will identify with an ambitious aspirational narrative – referred to within Habiforum as 'a dot on the horizon'. In practice, Habiforum conveners challenge the group to formulate and commit to extraordinary goals. They make sure that such high objectives are directly related to the area under development rather than reflecting the interests of specific parties. First they invite group members to tap into their individual passion, to express and share their dreams. Then they shepherd them through the process of consolidating their aspirations into a highly ambitious vision for the area. Facilitation is needed because participants find it difficult to transform the multitude of individual perspectives and intentions surrounding complex spatial-planning problems into a shared, ambitious vision that pushes everyone forward. Habiforum conveners are encouraged to help the group structure their conversation with plain but constructive 'how-can-we' questions. These types of questions spur the imagination while inviting stakeholders to incorporate others' interests into their creative thinking.

Committing to a highly ambitious collective vision rather than settling for a compromise takes time and effort, but it is necessary to get the buy-in of diverse stakeholders with competing priorities. It makes actors willing to engage seriously across boundaries and put their individual interests on hold for the time being. It signals the transition from a partial, discipline-based method to an integrated area-based approach. It is also critical later in motivating the group to keep on going when things get tough. This construction of a high aspirational narrative has to be inclusive, allowing participants to express and engage their identities in the development of the shared vision. It only ends when all individual group members have had their say and commit themselves personally to the endeavour.

Working together: everybody can be an initiator

Once a shared and ambitious objective has been articulated, conveners shift to the goal of working together to generate the best possible solutions. This involves sharing insights and experiences and freely exploring alternatives. It also involves experimenting with new solutions and initiating concrete transitions in the situation – developing entirely new 'genres' of practices when required. A key principle at this stage is that 'everybody can be an initiator'. This means that proposals for action steps can come from anyone, independent of function or status. By reifying power and boundaries and shielding the process from undue domination by traditional paradigms and players, Habiforum creates an open space in which all participants are equally invited to contribute to solutions. This principle has brought unknown professionals into leadership positions. For instance, farmers took leadership in re-imagining possibilities for the Overdiepse. Similarly, 'ordinary' local residents drove the transformation of the old railway workshop. When people saw that truly new practices were required and welcomed, they responded by becoming initiators no matter their status or position.

This stage often turns out to be the real test for a group. It gives an indication of the additional efforts a convener needs to make and whether to invite others to join. Once it works, the convening role changes. Some become more of a facilitator; others start to function as a normal group member; and others even leave the scene entirely.

These convening practices have a logical flow, but they are not strictly sequential. Conveners often move back and forth between them or apply them simultaneously. For example, the design of a solution or the launch of a pilot initiative may bring new insights into the situation or attract others who offer their help.

The role of conveners

There is no denying that the key ingredient in the success of Habiforum is the central role that conveners played, through their work, their personality, their skills, and their persistence. As director of the practice programme Ab acted as a kind of 'master' convener: much of his role consisted in inspiring others to act as conveners too. With no practical experience in the field of professional learning strategies Ab had few opinions or preconceived ideas on what could and could not work. Nor did he feel any urge to develop any approach himself.

> I don't consider myself an innovator but more a 'signaller' who has a very good feel for 'what's in the air'.

His experience in a government agency gave him some legitimacy, but he was not representing any organization or perspective. Ab now reflects that he kept too much distance and did not challenge others enough to make a difference beyond their projects. As a result too many people 'just did their own thing' without really committing themselves to a wider vision. Still his attitude drove him to invite practitioners from many different backgrounds and disciplines to leverage their expertise, reputation, or position. They were able to take the lead in convening others who could contribute innovative solutions to difficult challenges using a wide range of approaches. He promoted the concept of community of practice as a mode of convening that encouraged action-learning, collaboration, and experimentation across formal organizational and professional structures. Time and again he met with practitioners in the field to inspire them about the challenges Habiforum would be working on and the convening approach it had adopted. In addition to inviting practitioners, Ab also convinced many decision-makers to join Habiforum or get involved in one of its projects. He did not hesitate to leverage his position as a source of funding to push people to adopt a 'convening' attitude, for instance when he invited applicants to put in joint proposals as a consortium. Although a number of these consortia hardly made it through their first project, others developed into fruitful and long-lasting collaborations.

At a later stage, Ab convened a select group of Habiforum facilitators to explore the role of convener with them. He invested a lot of effort in connecting them and creating learning opportunities for them. At first he tried to form a community of practice among them, called 'the MetaCoP', to capture lessons across all projects. For a variety of reasons it did not work out. MetaCoP meetings were largely used to arrange practical things, report on progress of projects, and rarely got beyond that stage. The facilitators' exclusive focus on their own projects turned out to be an obstacle to combining insights and generating collective knowledge. As a result the meetings remained oriented to individual projects rather than developing a shared practice. After the MetaCoP came to an end, Ab initiated a series of focused meetings around specific topics.

Although the conversation among facilitators about their mutual experiences improved, the linkages across the group as a whole remained rather weak. The diversity of practitioners, approaches, and projects in Habiforum also had its downsides: the ample opportunities to experiment typical of Habiforum's way of working hindered the integration of outcomes. Building bridges across projects to link practitioners and experiments turned out to be one of the main challenges until the end of the programme. Ab now regards this lack of connection between projects as the main flaw in Habiforum. It is something to which he should have paid a lot more attention and about which he should have been more directive:

> We have established too few links between different experiments and practices, let alone between practitioners and the academic network. Experiments may have been too loosely connected and did not build upon each other. We should have challenged the associates more to do so.

A combination of intention, intuition, and openness seems to have been a key ingredient in getting the programme under way and sustaining it for ten years. As is typical for systems conveners there was always a lot of pressure from sponsoring governments and decision-makers who were looking for quick answers to the problems they faced. In spite of such pressure, Ab kept an open attitude throughout the project, refusing to settle for easy, but unsatisfactory, certainties. This seems to have played a crucial role in his success as a convener and his ability to inspire Habiforum's associates:

> To be honest, I did not have any clear ideas on where we had to go with the programme. All I knew was that current approaches failed to deal with the challenges we had in front of us and that we urgently needed to develop new ways of working in spatial planning. I was only aware that learning together was important but had no clue what the new practices we needed had to look like. And to be honest, that remained the case for many years.

The experience of Habiforum has had a profound effect on all who were involved, and on Ab most of all. Now he has co-initiated a new project, *Netherlands Above Water*, using the lessons of Habiforum to create coalitions and new practices in participative water management. It's hard to tell if being a convener is an irrepressible personal trait or a kind of addictive, adrenaline-inducing contact sport!

Notes

1. An article about this project appeared in the *New York Times*, February 13, 2013, entitled 'Going with the flow': http://www.nytimes.com/2013/02/17/arts/design/flood-control-in-the-netherlands-now-allows-sea-water-in.html?pagewanted=all (last accessed February 19, 2014).
2. Ab van Luin has a personal website called 'Spade' where he describes himself as a 'space maker and coalition builder. He helps . . . project teams, organizations and networks to allow for the formation of producing coalitions with people who want to make a difference space [sic]': http://www.spadenet.nl/over-spade.html. He offers 'Practice Learning . . . at the start of a project as teams of client and each to know, learning to work with new contract and/or in complex situations and sustainable working arrangement want to make with each other [sic]': http://www.spadenet.nl/praktijkleren.html.
3. For information about the series of community meetings, range of books, and website, see www.habiforum.nl and its successor www.nlbw.nl (in Dutch).

Chapter 8

The IDEA Partnership

Convening learning partnerships in the complex landscape of special education

Joanne Cashman, Patrice Cunniff Linehan, Mariola Rosser, Etienne Wenger-Trayner and Beverly Wenger-Trayner

Thirty-five years after a law was passed by the US Congress requiring states to provide adequate education to people with disabilities there are still wide gaps in the kinds of services offered to students with special educational needs. This chapter describes our efforts to convene learning partnerships among the different stakeholders involved. It is our belief that their coming together is essential for creating lasting change in the physical, academic, and social lives of all students.

The chapter begins with some background to the legislation and a description of the project that was funded to support implementation of this law. We then outline the challenges we faced in this project in terms of the complexity of the landscape of practice. Indeed, to form new learning partnerships in the service of people with disabilities, we are bringing together diverse stakeholders working in different sectors and at different levels of scale. To illustrate how the project operates we relate the three-part story of a community of practice realized at the federal, state, and local levels. Finally, we use these stories to reflect on our approach to convening in complex landscapes and draw out what we are learning from the experience.

The IDEA Partnership

In the mid-1970s, the United States Congress passed a piece of legislation called the *Individuals with Disabilities Education Act* (IDEA). This act requires states to provide 'free, appropriate, public education' to all individuals with disabilities. The legislation was a landmark at the time, and states have made great strides toward the law's goal of offering all students an appropriate educational program. Yet more than three decades after the enactment of the legislation, persistent academic and behavioral challenges remain. To fulfill the intent of the law, groups across the landscape must come together to make progress in changing practices around the physical, academic, and social needs of all students. For those who administer, implement, and are affected by the provisions of the IDEA, a shift toward more collaboration across systems is critical.

It was to this end that the *IDEA Partnership* was formed.[1] The IDEA Partnership is a long-term project funded at the federal level to support implementation of the law through a process of accelerated learning across relevant stakeholder groups,[2] a strategy that is instrumental for achieving real change in practice.

As systems conveners for the Partnership, we bring together disabled people, their families, counselors, educators, and health providers to work as partners with researchers, decision-makers, and technical assistance providers. The mission of the IDEA Partnership is threefold:

- Demonstrate the value of broad stakeholder engagement in influencing changes in practice.
- Use the networks that already exist in national organizations to build stakeholder engagement at national, state, and local levels.
- Bridge the boundaries that separate those who should be working together to achieve real inclusion for individuals with disabilities.

A landscape with multiple dimensions of complexity

The goal of providing adequate educational opportunities to all individuals with disabilities involves a great variety of practices on different sides of traditional boundaries. The IDEA Partnership works with over 50 national organizations, including groups that represent policymakers, administrators, practitioners, families, and youth.[3] We bring these groups into a working relationship with state agencies and local schools.

The complexity of this landscape reflects the following dimensions.

Multiple levels of scale

For our work to have real impact, learning needs to take place at multiple levels of scale at once. IDEA is a federal mandate with policies at the national level. Education in the US is the responsibility of each state: it is managed by education departments at the state level, administered by local school districts, and delivered in each school. The challenge is to enable learning at each level and to connect the different levels into meaningful learning partnerships. For instance, states can learn from each other's experience in implementing the federal mandate. Different agencies within state governments can learn to coordinate their work to serve the same children. Policymakers need to understand the effect of their policies on practice and on students. Conversely, practitioners and parents need opportunities to understand the intention behind the policies that affect them. In convening learning partnerships, we work across different levels of scale to include federal and state agencies, local districts, site leaders, practitioners, families, and youth.

Multiple domains

Learning needs to take place in a large number of potentially relevant domains. We have focused on several key domains, including transition from school to college and career; integration of school-based and community-based behavioral health; and the academic and behavioral barriers to achievement. For each domain, different groups have specific sets of related issues they care about. Domains are chosen because they cut across the system and offer unique opportunities to form new learning partnerships and build broad commitment to transform practice.

Multiple sources of knowledge

We find that people look to trusted sources for information and guidance. Both formal and informal sources exist. Formal sources use policy statements and an evidence base grounded in research, while informal sources derive knowledge from practice. While these can reflect differences in power, both are important components of knowledgeability. We believe the success of our partnerships depends on recognizing the role that each can play in moving collective learning forward.

Multiple sources of authority

Because IDEA entails legal requirements, individuals look to recognized sources of authority for setting the directions and boundaries for action. In a federal system of education, certain provisions are required for all by federal law, but states can add additional provisions. In turn, districts can move beyond state regulation in creating their own local policies. Relevant sources of authority exist at each level of scale. For important issues of practice, the right level of scale is not always apparent and progress usually depends on leveraging sources of authority at multiple levels.

Multiple sources of influence

While authority is important in shaping behavior, people also respond to their own insights and the insights of trusted colleagues in making their decisions about how to behave. In our learning partnerships, influential groups include professional associations in general education as well as in special education, family advocates, and youth leaders. Influential groups often have national organizations as well as local chapters.

Multiple stakeholders

Education involves a wide array of participants and stakeholders. Some, like state agencies, have authority through policy and monitoring. Others, such as professional associations and advocacy groups, have influence through their deep and durable networks of members. Many others affect outcomes through direct engagement with students. Involving all types of stakeholders in a learning partnership is key to achieving sustainable changes in practice.

All these dimensions of complexity intersect in our efforts to engage all the relevant partners around critical issues.

Communities of practice at multiple levels of scale

Our convening strategy has been to start by cultivating communities of practice for a few key domains. These communities are broad and long-lived enough to call on people's identities and serve as a context for the various learning partnerships and focused activities we facilitate. One of the most important and enduring examples of such a community convened by the IDEA Partnership is the National Community of Practice on School Behavioral Health.

Behavioral health is an issue that concerns individuals across systems and from an array of disciplines. The domain focuses on emotional support for youth in school and in their community. Over time, a flurry of initiatives have sprung up to address this issue, led by education, health, mental health, and family groups. Each initiative has its own brand, targeted leverage points, set of supporters, and unique vocabulary. Some are based in schools and some in the community, but they often serve the same populations. Few crosswalks exist to connect related initiatives, although many are complementary and some are completely aligned.

Complex and multi-scale, this collaboration between different stakeholders in the area of behavioral health has challenged our ability to convene and facilitate and continues to energize us today. Their story is a good illustration of the kind of convening we try to do.

We tell this story in three parts, showing how the collaboration has manifested itself at the national, state, and local levels. The first story is about the *national* community of practice on school behavioral health. The next two focus on Hawaii and Pennsylvania, two of several states involved in the national community that went on to form similar communities of practice at the *state* level. In the Pennsylvania case, we highlight the example of a school district that brought together public and private partners to work on behavioral health issues at a *local* level.

Launching the national community of practice on school behavioral health

The community of practice on school behavioral health has its roots in the *Shared Agenda* (Policymaker Partnership 2002), an initiative that was co-sponsored in

2001 by the National Association of Mental Health Program Directors and the National Association of State Directors of Special Education. Through the IDEA Partnership fifty stakeholders representing national, state, local, and individual interests were brought together to explore potential collaboration across the school–community divide.

Then in 2004 one hundred stakeholders were brought together by the IDEA Partnership and the national Center for School Mental Health to build on the cross-boundary relationships defined in the Shared Agenda. To help facilitate the dialogue, trigger people's imagination, and align the perspectives of different stakeholders, the meeting was structured by four key questions we have devised as a framework for bringing people together:

• Who cares about this issue and why?
• What work is under way separately to address this issue?
• What productive endeavor would unite us in doing real work?
• How we can build the connections?

The discussions that ensued were lively and diverse. They helped ground a context for ongoing engagement to address common challenges, involve potential partners, seek a shared language, and align major funding streams. The joint commitment from this meeting gave birth to the National Community of Practice on School Behavioral Health.

I have been able to use this venue to participate in developing a family-driven definition of family engagement in response to an outside request [from a national committee]. As an occupational therapist, this community of practice even connected me to others in my discipline who were also working on how we contribute to school mental health.

(A local practitioner, active member of her professional organization and the national community)

Since then the national community has grown to include 16 states with cross-agency teams, 21 national organizations, and 11 federally funded technical assistance centers. They meet annually in person and monthly by teleconference to define priority issues that can make a national impact. The community has spawned 12 'practice groups' focused on specific issues such as the connections between school-wide positive behavioral interventions and mental health; mental health and the transition from school to post-school; and behavioral health from cradle to college and career. Several states in the national community have been showcased by federal agencies as exemplars of cross-agency work.

The community's annual conference attracts over 1,000 people. It is organized by the practice groups, which sponsor learning activities focused on a priority issue. They distribute the request for proposals, receive the submissions, rate the proposed sessions, and hold conference calls with the selected presenters. Practice group facilitators invite new members to breakfast and lunch sessions to explain the work of the group. With each successive conference, membership in the practice groups has grown as meeting attendees become community members. During the annual meeting, held in conjunction with the conference, the national community and each practice group set a work scope and place their activities on a shared calendar. The calendar makes the breadth of the community's work transparent, invites participation, sets critical timing, and provides an opportunity for practice groups to learn about and participate in each other's work. This has become a way to continuously explore issues and perspectives within the landscape of behavioral health.

Building a state community of practice in Hawaii

The national community has spawned communities at the state level. For more than a decade, policymakers in Hawaii had been pursuing the integration of education and mental health services to improve the wellbeing and achievement of children and youth. Much of the interest in working across state agencies was driven by litigation and the resulting federal court order that required, among many things, extensive examination and monitoring by federal agencies.

By the spring of 2005, it appeared that, after years of intervention, Hawaii was ready to steer its own system. The last federal monitoring report stated that the infrastructure was in place to deliver a system of school-based behavioral health alternatives and that measurable progress toward goals would continue.

To the leadership of the Hawaii Office of Special Education, it was clear that this high standard was not likely to be achieved through monitoring alone. Monitoring was a valuable technical process, but stopped short of addressing the dynamic relationships that undergird the system.

> We look to experts for guidance, but we must believe that the answers to our problems lie with us: what we know, what we learn, and what we choose to do.
> (A state CoP leader in Hawaii)

Learning partnerships within a community of practice offered a way for state agencies to engage local service providers and connect with the families and youth who were the intended beneficiaries.

Later that year, modeling the strategies promoted by the national community, the state Department of Education convened a meeting with other agencies and 50 diverse stakeholders to formalize partnerships in a statewide community of practice. State agency personnel wanted to create a working relationship among decision-makers, practitioners, and consumers. In this way, they could test their assumptions, create and evaluate pilot efforts, gain insights that could inform policy choices, and drive a strategy built on a shared vision.

> Adults can change, but we have to help them.
> (A local youth leader at Honoka'a High School in the North Hawaii CoP)

Today, the partnerships within the Hawaiian community of practice continue to flourish. Each island has established a local community and their representatives meet to strengthen the state community of practice through a number of learning partnerships that address cross-island issues.

Community councils, formed through the Department of Education, have become the backbone of the community of practice structure. Each island has its own priorities, and a leadership team works across islands to encourage stakeholder work on the issues they have identified as a priority.

Several local communities of practice have launched initiatives that have a broader impact. On the island of Oahu, for example, the community of practice worked with Families as Allies to launch campaigns to foster resiliency. The campaign, 'Make a Friend – Be a Friend', won a national award for family leadership. On the Big Island, North Hawaii youth inspired people at a national conference with a presentation of their student-to-student program, Ka'euepna (The Net), designed to help vulnerable students transition to high school and grow as youth advocates.

The leadership of the state community of practice continually model cross-boundary learning partnerships by aligning their support for work across departments. In 2012, 500 participants joined in a Summit sponsored by the Departments of Education and Health to pursue the future of behavioral health in Hawaii.

Working across public and private partners in Pennsylvania

Like many of the state teams in the national community of practice on behavioral health, Pennsylvania was interested in bridging the gap between school-based behavior support services and individual interventions delivered by community-based mental health professionals for individuals with significant behavior problems. At the time an evidence-based program, Positive Behavioral Supports and Interventions (PBIS), was being promoted in schools nationwide. The national community of practice agreed that local implementation of PBIS could significantly reduce the number of behavior issues in schools and create a more positive school climate for all students, but especially students with emotional disabilities. Through the state community of practice, the Pennsylvania Departments of Education and Public Welfare, along with a number of private partners, pooled resources and in-kind services to staff and implement PBIS.

While the primary work of the community of practice focused on implementing school-wide PBIS, some of the partners wondered if higher intensity needs might also be addressed through the collaboration of school and community partners. As a result, several demonstration projects were installed throughout the state.

One of the demonstration sites was the Scranton School District. In Scranton, as in many localities, education and mental health entities had loose connections but did not deeply integrate their missions, goals, and strategies. Inspired by the school/community partnerships established through the state community of practice, Scranton increasingly aligned their community services with school-wide efforts. The managed care provider serving the Scranton area realized the value of working on both prevention and intervention in schools with significant needs. Several community mental health workers were assigned full-time to the schools. Together with school leadership and staff they built a comprehensive program of school service and home/community carryover. Services that were once delivered in separate and discrete models are now planned and supported through joint initiatives encouraged by the state community of practice and managed by local agencies, private providers, and the school district.

Another district, Pocono Mountain, strategized about how to increase local capacity to address the needs of students that were being served in settings outside the school district. By working with the state community of practice and collaboratively across school staff and local providers, they were able to build the skills necessary to serve students in the district. Funded by the Department of Special Education the state community of practice initiated a 'return on investment' (ROI) study and determined that the district built new capacity while saving over $135,000.

Statewide, among the schools partnering in the PBIS effort, out-of-school suspension days were reduced by 35.2 percent in the first two years. Academic achievement rates for school sites implementing the framework with fidelity increased at a rate higher than the state average. By the 2011–12 school year, more than 300 schools and 50 early childhood centers were served without a dedicated funding stream from any agency. Today, over 400 schools participate in the PBIS work managed by the twenty-seven public and private partners in the community of practice. The strong connection between local partnerships and Pennsylvania's state community of practice increases the likelihood that policy discussions held in state agencies will reflect the realities of local practice. Likewise, Pennsylvania's participation in the national community of practice ensures that practice advancements are communicated to states, national organizations, and federal agencies with similar challenges and a shared commitment to behavioral health.

Convening as an approach to learning

The goal of the IDEA Partnership is to accelerate learning by forming new partnerships across the landscape and addressing shared challenges together. Our efforts are guided by a few basic principles we believe can bring about sustainable change in practice:

- Individuals at all levels are more open to information and influence from groups with which they voluntarily affiliate.
- Through structured interaction to work on concrete issues, individuals can discover shared interests that go beyond their different roles and organizational positions.

- Real change in practice requires learning partnerships that include decision-makers who are responsible for policies and programs as well as individuals who both implement and are served by those programs.

Learning through shared work

The initial barriers are significant. Potential partners have successfully operated in their current structure for years. There is something to be gained but also something at risk for most potential partners. Professional organizations have long histories of leadership on specific issues; state agencies have a mandate to implement; and advocacy groups have a passion for the 'consumer' perspective. Often there is a history of mistrust or blame among them. Yet, the appeal of broader support, easier access to information, and recognition as an important contributor all pique their interest. The right mix of people and strategies, with some early gains, is essential to keep their interest and catalyze further participation.

Our basic approach is to engage partners in doing actual work together, for instance understanding the implications of a piece of legislation or crafting a response to a policy. Usually, this is work they would have to do anyway to pursue the agenda of their own organizations, but which they can do better together. The goal is not to replace individual agendas with new ones, but to explore the commonalities across agendas. This shared work is a way to achieve some early progress that has immediate value for the new partners. It also provides the infrastructure for building relationships that are likely to create value in the future.

Complex landscape, simple questions

We have developed a simple strategy for finding a workable entry point into the complexity of the landscape and getting the buy-in of diverse stakeholders. Given an issue we need to address, we begin by identifying potential partners in the landscape and then articulate the issue as expressed by those partners. This process is structured by the four simple questions mentioned earlier in the story:

- Who cares about this issue and why?
- What work is under way separately to address this issue?
- What productive endeavor would unite us in doing real work together?
- How can we build the connections?

> I saw [the Partnership] begin with nothing but just a few ideas and I really saw it transform the way people interact with each other. I saw it bring respect for the various organizations [and their positions] from organizations that probably did not respect each other to start with. And I saw it reduce some of the fear that you saw among professional organizations toward the parent organizations. Those things are still worth doing, very much so.
>
> (A national leader)

These questions help to ground the context for facilitating interactions: common issues, potential partners, boundaries, differences in vocabulary to express common themes, as well as areas for shared work, common messages, venues for joint communications, and opportunities for aligning major funding streams. Potential partners have diverse but important contributions to make. Convening them for exchange, joint exploration, and shared work becomes the key strategy.

Communities of practice as an infrastructure for collaborative learning

School behavioral health is one example of a successful and enduring community of practice, but the Partnership facilitates a constellation of interconnected communities, each with state-level communities and national practice groups. We facilitate these communities very intentionally through annual meetings, regular community calls, activities and projects sponsored by practice groups, state-to-state sharing, and a customized website that supports online collaboration (www.sharedwork.org).

When states and organizations are joined in such a sustained community, we find that the identification that develops over time supports the spread of successful strategies and the creation of new knowledge. A national community invites the development of state communities, which likewise invite the development of local ones. At the local level, people closest to the work join with each other and connect with the state community to learn what will advance and constrain changes in practice. In this way, state agencies develop more enlightened policy and guidance grounded in the realities of practice. Conversely, stakeholders develop a deeper understanding of the driving forces behind state policy choices. The gap between 'knowing' and 'doing' (Pfeiffer and Sutton, 2000) starts to close as issues are pursued in active and collective ways. Information, tools, and innovation are transferred from colleague to colleague faster and with relevance. Documents from research, policy, and practice gain meaning as they are discussed and translated into practice by community members. Last but not least, such productive experiences of social learning progressively change how people behave in the Partnership and beyond.

New habits of interaction, new identities

Trust is critical for crossing enduring boundaries of practice, affiliation, agencies, roles, and perspectives; but it is a process that takes time and persistence. We find that trust develops in a learning partnership when it has been reinforced over time – on a range of issues – and when relationships have been useful in negotiating a variety of challenges. The trust that develops over time through such shared work becomes a foundation for crossing real and imagined boundaries.

One of our goals is to help people discover the value of this type of deep collaborative learning. This requires them to practice new 'habits of interaction.' Over the years, we have developed a framework to foster these habits. Its four components form the basis for our work and, together with the infrastructure we create, define our approach to convening learning partnerships in landscapes of practice:

Coalescing around issues – Grounded in the range of perspectives, we encourage the search for shared concerns, asking: What will bring people together? Where do the multiple perspectives on this issue begin to diverge? Where is there potential for alignment? How can we leverage the information/activity that already exists? How will we frame this issue for shared work?

Ensuring relevant participation – Challenging the habits of shallow collaboration, we encourage the partners to reach out and get the right mix of stakeholders, asking: Who must be involved to ensure changes in practice? What will ensure that decision-makers, practitioners, and consumers have an active role? What tools and communication vehicles will support engagement?

Doing work together – We believe that engagement in shared work deepens relationships and convinces people of the value of engaging beyond their comfort zone. We pose these questions: How will relationships and activities advance shared work and learning? What individual goals will be met through doing work together? What collective goals will be met through doing work together?

Leading by convening – With a focus on sharing leadership and leveraging the connections that each stakeholder brings, we encourage partners to reflect: Can individuals in all roles become leaders in learning? How can we translate complex challenges into ways that individuals can contribute? How can individuals support learning by acting as conveners within their own networks?[4]

Figure 8.1 summarizes our approach to leading by convening. The middle row describes areas in which our partnerships promote collaboration: technical areas where challenges can be addressed with the right information or expert advice, adaptive areas, where challenges need human negotiation for accommodation to different situations, and operational areas where decision-making requires a mix of technical and adaptive approaches.[5] The bottom row describes progressive levels of depth of collaboration that our partners recognized in their interactions, from merely informing each other about their respective positions, to connecting with each other, to working together on joint challenges, and ultimately to transforming their respective practices.[6]

It has been said that the difficult task is not acquiring a new habit but giving up the old one. In many ways this adage applies to agencies, organizations, and individuals as they enter learning partnerships. Our approach to sharing leadership on important issues is a significant departure from current practice, even

Leading by Convening

Habits of the interaction		
Coalescing around issues	Ensuring relevant participation	Doing the work together

Elements of the interaction		
Adaptive	Technical	Operational

Depth of the interaction			
Informing	Networking	Collaborating	Transforming

Figure 8.1 Dimensions of leading by convening

for those who would describe themselves as collaborative or knowledgeable about the landscape.

Deep collaborations, boundary crossing, and trying to make a difference in the landscape as a whole require 'identity' work (Wenger, 2007). To help our partners build their new identities as collaborators in the landscape, we need to continually provide learning opportunities that demonstrate the difference, help individuals to value deeper collaboration, and expand their knowledgeability of the landscape. As suggested in Chapter 6, proposing new identities involves all three modes of identification. To achieve this, people have to re-imagine themselves as connected to the whole landscape. They have to learn to engage with others in new ways. And they have to realign their work so that it contributes to a broader vision of what is possible. When the three aspects combine, they progressively see themselves as actors in the landscape. Believing that one can initiate and sustain change is a key piece of making change possible. Complexity hinders opportunities to see and believe one can make a difference. Crossing the boundaries that separate people who do related work gives them a new sense of their field of action. Such transformation of identity happens over time, but it ends up driving thought and behavior across situations. We have found that the repeated experience of deep collaboration transforms individuals and gradually changes the way they collaborate, not only in the context of our Partnership, but also in their own organizations and agencies.

This work is long term. Our Partnership enjoys a foundation of relationships that have been built across more than 50 partners over 13 years. This foundation

> The Partnership . . . gave me hope to feel that I could really impact systems change as an individual who believes in systems change. They have given me the tools, the support and the mentoring to take my work to another level.
>
> (A national partner)

enables us to invite partners into a range of learning opportunities around difficult issues. With each invitation, the connections deepen, the coherence becomes clearer, habits of collaboration are reinforced, and people develop new identities oriented to the landscape.

Convening roles in a complex landscape of practice

Our experience through the IDEA Partnership has made us more aware of the variety of roles conveners must play. The following roles define the parameters in which we operate as conveners, using our knowledge of the partners and their contexts to create opportunities.

The sensing role: continuously identify the current organizational agendas and emerging interests that allow cross-stakeholder interaction. Facilitation of a complex venture like the IDEA Partnership requires the ability to sense potential connections by taking the perspective of relevant organizations and anticipating the forces that could drive and constrain collaboration. We find that it is an essential role for encouraging and facilitating open interchange among partners. Over time, partners appreciate the value of such sensing behavior: they begin to identify new partners and see how to invite them into the work.

The brokering role: facilitate interactions that build shared understanding across contexts. In a learning partnership, value does not come from the ability to collect and distribute information, but rather to make information personally meaningful. Many programs exist to collect and distribute information. The point is to leverage relationships and convene learning activities to help people select, organize, and make sense of information in ways that are relevant to their own contexts. In the Partnership, this brokering across boundaries takes place at two levels: bringing a wider group of partners into an existing activity and making strategic use of the networks that each partner has in place to create a multiplier effect.

The modeling role: consistently model cross-stakeholder work in all undertakings. The participatory approach we advance appears idealistic to some stakeholders. More straightforward strategies seem to offer more predictability and often have greater appeal. Therefore, every activity must demonstrate the concrete value added through cross-stakeholder work. Every instance of Partnership collaboration is held to that standard: to challenge the common wisdom; to help people leave their old habits of episodic and shallow collaboration; and in particular to include as participants and leaders in the work under-represented groups, such as families, individuals with cultural and linguistic differences, and youth with disabilities. Consistent modeling is an effective strategy for change, especially when coupled with a set of tools to plan, structure, and reflect on Partnership activities.

> In over 20 years of advocacy work, I have never felt more like a partner than when I am working through the CoP.
>
> (A family advocate member of a state CoP leadership team)

The coaching role: support partners in practicing a more collaborative approach in their own networks. The Partnership is committed to helping states and organizations value and meet a high standard for collaboration. We find that new connections and frequent participation in activities that yield results around high-value issues are critical to building a personal identity as a collaborator and learning partner. Therefore, we invest in activities that help partners build their 'identity' as collaborators. In many cases this means that we contribute to activities in their context, by supporting them, making connections, or even participating directly.

The designing role: build the infrastructure for sustainable work through national and state-based communities of practice and electronic networking. The types of broad and complex communities of practice we rely on as a context for facilitating learning partnerships do not develop without intentional cultivation. Most obviously, the increasing demand for guiding tools and technology infrastructure requires us to take a designing role. But the design role is pervasive. Finding the right rhythm of interaction among the right partners is essential to advancing the work and building the relationships, and it requires careful planning. Even ensuring that all stakeholders have a sense of ownership and an opportunity to take leadership needs to be part of an intentional design, especially given the differences in power that characterize the landscape.

The reflecting role: establish a data collection and evaluation system that documents activities, conditions for success, and has an impact. While communities of practice are receiving significantly more attention as a strategy in education today, there are still many skeptics.[7] The approach is far less linear than traditional implementation designs. Therefore, we are under pressure to show impact and we have to balance the short-terms expectations of

> I was really with a lot of people who were doing the same thing and some were ahead of me and helped me. There is an immediate acceptance of people who participate in the process. You're made to feel as though you are part of the process and a significant contributing member.
>
> (A partner from a national organization)

organizations with the long-term needs of the network. To answer this challenge, the Partnership has established an array of quantitative and qualitative metrics that help us document claims of value. The formative evaluation team including staff, evaluation contractors, and partner leaders collect and analyze the data in response to the formal measures requested by our funder. Case studies focus on value-creation stories that account for the immediate, potential, and realized value the Partnership contributes (as defined in Wenger et al., 2011). Value-creation stories encourage reflection and describe how participation has helped community members redefine their work and shape their future interactions. As systems conveners who manage an array of tasks, we find that reflection and evaluation must be built into our routine. Nothing short of an ongoing commitment to data collection, evaluation, and storytelling can demonstrate the impact of learning together. This is especially important for a long-term project where the context is shifting and new participants and sponsors need to be brought on board.

Each of these roles entails a number of specific behaviors. To some conveners they come naturally; others need more help. In the IDEA Partnership, we have been increasingly attentive to these behaviors: identifying them and creating simple tools such as question sets, discussion protocols, and guidebooks to enable others to grow as conveners. Tools help, but cannot replace the credibility and personal relationships developed through common work.

Looking back and moving forward

In this chapter, we have mostly described how the Partnership operates and what we do to help it work. But social learning is not linear. Even well-planned and supported efforts struggle to achieve all that conveners envision. Such is the experience in our Partnership as well. While we describe exemplary efforts in some states, others struggle to maintain cohesion and deal with frequent changes in leadership. We are able to offer quotes from members who have found personal and professional value, but we know many more would engage if we could find the right mix of issues and activities to involve them. Even though we have been at it for many years and have made much headway, ours is still a work in progress. We continue to learn every day and through every new relationship. Some lessons do reappear often enough to be worth offering by way of conclusion:

- Looking for the multiple dimensions of an issue is critical to drawing in the right partners. Surely, learning partnerships demand focus, but the pressure to focus must not constrict our full examination. We risk an incomplete picture of the problem if we ignore the multiple perspectives that shape the work around an issue of concern. Often, we must translate concepts from the terminology of one discipline to another to help discover the commonalities. As described in Chapter 1, accountability and expressibility must be in balance. Conveners need to be able to sense differences and make it safe to express differences, all the while holding the group accountable to its aspirations.
- Learning partnerships that have the most value for widespread changes in practice across levels of scale. Over time, multi-scale partnerships nurture the relationships that have been missing in bridging research and policy with practice. Of course, we can learn with peers at the same level of the system. Yet, the learning partnerships that have the most promising outcomes are ones that reflect the location of any practice in broader systems. In our domain, implementation has federal, state, and local components. When a learning partnership fosters potential leadership across levels of scale, the full set of perspectives yields more encompassing strategies and draws more widespread support.

- While we value the multi-scale aspects of learning partnerships, coherence and alignment across the domain is also important. Negotiating agendas, examining longitudinal implications, and mapping current and emerging connections are key strategies that conveners must develop. To maintain legitimacy in a complex environment, conveners must think beyond their own funding streams and mandates. We often find ourselves helping people move beyond the specificities of their own language to an underlying purpose.
- Of our early lessons, one stands out as the most valuable: honor the work that has come before the current undertaking. Don't ask anyone to give up their own 'framework.' Instead, ask them to seek commonality and find value in both their own *and* the larger agenda.

For the IDEA Partnership, as with all conveners, the learning goes on. Our daily work is energized by the knowledge that we are part of a larger group of individuals who are simultaneously acting in these roles and willing to share the lessons learned in developing our own identities as collaborators and conveners.

Notes

1. For ease of reading in this chapter we will use capitalized Partnership to refer to the IDEA Partnership and lowercase partnership for the general term.
2. More specifically, the IDEA Partnership is a project funded by the Office of Special Education Programs (OSEP). It is one of a number of targeted investments designed to deliver information and support implementation of the law by advancing the use of research and evidence-based practice. Yet, the Partnership has a unique purpose: it is specifically funded to build connections between federal investments, national organizations, and state education agencies. Our work focuses on the human aspects that can impact the spread and use of the evidence-based practices dominating federally sponsored technical assistance programs. To date, our work has been funded for 14 years through successive investments that are five years in duration. With each funding cycle, the learning, the relationships, and the outcomes have reshaped the continuing investment.
3. Collectively, the 50+ Partnership organizations reach over 7 million stakeholders.
4. As we struggled to put those habits into a framework that others might use, we turned to the foreword written by Etienne Wenger as an introduction to our manual for state agencies. His description of our efforts through the lens of his work in social learning allowed us to see and express the values we hold as we begin to convene groups and enable others to convene and facilitate groups of their own (Wenger, 2007).
5. The distinction between technical and adaptive challenges comes from the work of Heifetz and Linsky in their book, *Leadership on the Line* (2002). The operational area was added by our partners.
6. Our approach to leading by convening is further elaborated in a practical guide *Leading by Convening: A Blueprint for Authentic Engagement* (December 2013), available online at www.ideapartnership.org.
7. The situation has changed over the last few years. Many education reformers now believe that a 'communities of practice' approach is a promising strategy to address the

persistent problem of bringing successful initiatives 'to scale' (U.S. Department of Education, 2009). With the heightened importance of sharing knowledge across organizational boundaries, the concept is now being applied by the federal government in many areas.

References

Heifetz, R. & Linsky, M. (2002). *Leadership on the Line*. Boston: Harvard Business Review Press.

IDEA Partnership (2013). *Leading by Convening: A Blueprint for Authentic Engagement* (December 2013), available online at www.ideapartnership.org

Pfeffer, J. & Sutton, R. I. (2000). *The Knowing–Doing Gap*. Boston: Harvard Business School Press.

Policymaker Partnership (2002). *Toward a Shared Agenda*. Alexandria, VA: National Association of State Directors of Special Education.

U.S. Department of Education (2009). *Race to the Top Program: Executive Summary*. Retrieved from www2.ed.gov/programs/racetothetop/executive-summary.pdf on September 4, 2012.

Wenger, E. (2007) in Cashman, J., Linehan, P., & Rosser, M. *Communities of Practice: A new approach to solving complex educational problems*. Alexandria, VA: National Association of State Directors of Special Education, x–xi.

Wenger, E., Trayner, B., & de Laat, M. (2011). *Promoting and Assessing Value Creation in Communities and Networks: A Conceptual Framework*. The Netherlands: Ruud de Moor Centrum, Open University of the Netherlands.

Part IV

Conclusions, and an invitation to a continued conversation

Chapter 9

Challenges for practice-based education

Mark Fenton-O'Creevy, Steven Hutchinson, Chris Kubiak, Beverly Wenger-Trayner and Etienne Wenger-Trayner

The inquiry that led to this book was prompted by questions about practice-based professional learning. This book is not the endpoint of our inquiry. Rather we framed it as an invitation to a conversation. By way of conclusion, we offer some thoughts about implications we have drawn for our own work and issues we are still wrestling with.

While we focus our reflections on practice-based learning, they are likely to have resonance with broader questions about higher education, concerning lifelong learning, employability, assessment, and the role of the university. These questions are generating a lot of thinking and innovation directed at the future of higher education. Our reflections are offered as contributions to these conversations.

Practice-based learning in landscapes of practice

Our framework suggests a view of students (and faculty) on a learning trajectory through a landscape of practice. These learning travellers have to find their way into and around specific practices, build an image of where these practices are located in the landscape, engage with multiple places in the landscape at once, cross boundaries, and develop an identity that is resilient and productive. From this perspective, key educational questions are:

- What experiences do students gain of the landscapes they will inhabit from their journey through higher education?
- How can these experiences transform who they are and propel them on a productive lifelong learning trajectory?
- What does this perspective mean for the professional development of academic faculty?

Identity work

Throughout the book we have presented identity as subject to frequent challenges and disruption. Moving across the landscape and learning at its boundaries requires identity work – revising, maintaining, and strengthening a sense of self as coherent and distinctive whilst negotiating identity and aligning with differing regimes of competence in different parts of the landscape. The role of identity work in learning has received considerable attention in recent decades; in scholarly work on higher education and practice-based learning.[1] However, in this book, we have highlighted some aspects of identity work that we believe deserve more attention:

- the challenges of developing resilient and dynamic identities in relation to multiple communities of practice;
- the emotional consequences of threats to identity engendered by perceptions of failure and incompetence in transitions across boundaries;
- the provisional and temporary nature, for many learners, of their engagement and alignment with academic practices.

Faculty identities and online learning

In designing a course on online learning for faculty members from around the world, we spent time listening to their concerns. Whilst online learning is seen as strategically important by the leaders of the majority of universities, many of their faculty continue to have deep concerns about the implications for their work (Allen & Seaman, 2013).

Many of these concerns are, at their heart, concerns about academic identity. For example, many experience shifts towards online modes of learning as asking them to move from an identity of subject expert to an identity of expert in learning design and learning technologies. Other fear a loss of academic freedom (a core facet of academic identity) under the pressures to use course designs and materials produced by others, or to surrender control of the learning materials they produce.

In designing the programme, we took care to engage with the emotions generated by these issues. We provided space for participants to reflect on their own emotional reactions, and those of their colleagues, to the demands to become a different kind of academic.

While the programme tries to take a broad view of the system-wide change being enacted in their landscapes of practice, it also emphasizes the emotional interplay of identity work and identity regulation in these arenas.

This approach is not without difficulties. Whilst many find it valuable and unusual to have the space to engage with these issues, some have significant concerns about the expressibility of their emotional selves in a workshop concerned with professional practice. One participant told us 'being asked about my emotional reaction to all this brought me up short. That's my personal life. I don't think it has any place in discussions about teaching practices.'

The challenge for the facilitators is to create a setting related to but separate from the professional domain in which such concerns about challenges to identity and competence, and the sometimes difficult emotions they arouse, become safely expressible.

What is the role of educational programmes in supporting such identity work? If deep learning involves identity work that can be disturbing, then how do we include resilience-building experiences in the core of the curriculum?

Boundaries

Sometimes it can seem as though universities conspire to obscure boundaries in the landscape rather than explicitly recognizing them as sites for learning. Certainly boundaries can seem invisible to a student. Consider the MBA student who told one of us the following story:

> I signed up for an MBA to learn how to be a senior manager. So I figured that the material I was learning was pretty much how senior managers talk among themselves. Well I was a year into my [part-time] course and I had to do a presentation to the senior team in our firm. I worked really hard at working ideas and frameworks from my course into the presentation. The day came and five minutes into my spiel, the MD leaned back in his chair waved his hand at the screen and said 'What is all this bollocks? Talk English for Christ's sake!' I was pretty shocked. In the end it wasn't career threatening but it was a pretty uncomfortable experience.

Boundaries are a challenge for practice-based education in three ways. First is the boundary between work and educational settings. Second are boundaries among academic disciplines relevant to one's trajectory. Third are boundaries in the students' own landscape, among work practices, management, policy-making, and the practices of their clients. All three present significant challenges to both understanding and identity.

How do we leverage these boundaries as learning assets? Can we help students use significant boundaries to deepen their understanding of the landscape and possibly become brokers across some of these boundaries?

Many programmes around the world are attempting to bridge boundaries with approaches such as problem-based and experiential learning.

At the University of Hong Kong an initiative is placing what they call 'experiential learning' at the heart of the university's pedagogy. Under this initiative, students conduct concrete projects in their area of study, run by the university for their pedagogical and social value – for instance, building a school in a rural area. Students become involved in all aspects of the projects, from planning to realization. They face the full complexity of an actual project including its practical, social, technical, and ethical dimensions. The initiative organizes learning, not merely as the transmission of a formal curriculum, but as the transformative growth of full human beings as they enter a field. The university is not just seeking to give students a bit of practical experience as is often done with internships. The central use of actual, meaningful projects aims to make experiential learning an integral part of the core curriculum. The initiative has started in professional schools, such as engineering, architecture, and business. Eventually, the vision is to adopt the approach across the university and adapt it to every discipline.

Competence and knowledgeability

Managing the complexity of the twenty-first century requires a subtle mix of competence and knowledgeability. This is true of graduate employability, which requires the ability to bring multiple perspectives to bear on problems. It is also true of citizenship and life more generally.

Much of the debate about developing the employability of university graduates has focused on the development of a range of generic skills. In many cases programmes to develop these skills are bolted on to university curricula; less often they are woven into the core curriculum. More sophisticated accounts of employability note the importance of adapting knowledge to new situations. Such accounts tend to recognize the problem of transferring university learning into the workplace.[2]

Taking knowledgeability seriously suggests new possibilities for conceptualizing employability. If we move from a focus solely on producing discipline-specific competence to supporting students in developing competence and knowledgeability across a landscape of practice, different concerns and challenges come into focus. This includes reflecting on the location of academic practices in the landscape. It also includes a focus on the development of workplace identities, the appropriate modulation of identity between different settings, and sensitivity to differences in the ways in which competence is judged in different settings. Such a perspective also suggests the value of approaches to employability that develop the relationships of engagement, imagination, and alignment with key practices in relevant landscapes of practice.

Some approaches to employability and practice-based learning already provide a potential platform for such an approach.

The Manchester Leadership Programme at the University of Manchester is a highly regarded and innovative cross-faculty programme which is a free choice option for many undergraduate students, built into programmes of study for some qualifications. It combines volunteering opportunities with team-based investigations into real organizations and individuals currently offering leadership on social issues (for example, leaders of social campaigns and movements or community leaders). Whilst course information emphasizes its role in developing core generic skills, it is a programme which requires students to navigate landscapes of practice in areas such as social campaigning and social policy and to integrate field investigations with academic ideas and frameworks.

In another degree programme for police officers, students were required to spend time in shelters for homeless people.

Such programmes could provide a platform for students to begin to grapple with and understand the challenges posed by developing knowledgeability across a landscape of practice.

Of course, many courses have embedded work placements, industry projects or work-based learning elements. All too often, however, these elements have little direct connection to the academic curriculum save through a written assessment which asks students to relate their project or learning to a set of academic frameworks. The difficulties of incommensurable ways of understanding the world or of expressing an appropriate identity in different contexts, or of experiencing incompetence in the transition to a new setting are glossed over or treated as peripheral to the learning experience. A focus on developing knowledgeability as a foundation for employability would bring these issues centre stage.

A focus on knowledgeability also provides a different perspective on assessment practices. Different and competing accountabilities to different parts of a landscape of practice and their different regimes of competence can often be obscured in educational assessment processes or treated as a needless complication; for example, the different perspectives of faculty and workplace mentors in a work-based learning or internship programme. A focus on developing knowledgeability grounds these differences and addresses the learner's need to navigate and negotiate these complexities. In this context, the different perspectives of representatives from different parts of the landscape become less a problem to be surmounted than a resource to be drawn on in developing and assessing the learner's knowledgeability.

Boud & Falchikov (2007) have noted the importance of students developing their own judgement about what constitutes good work. However, from a knowledgeability perspective, it is not enough for learners to develop their judgement about what constitutes good academic performance. They also need to develop their judgement about what constitutes good performance in the different parts of the landscapes of practice they travel and inhabit, and to develop a sense of why good practice is seen differently from different perspectives. The account in Chapter 5 of constructing a team around the student suggests an interesting way forward for practice-based learning. Such teams offer not just the opportunity to represent the professional landscape more fully in the learning process; they also generate more authentic modes of assessment. These modes of assessment address cross-landscape knowledgeability rather than simply competence within an academic genre or within a particular set of professional practices.

How do we design learning experiences that balance competence and knowledgeability? How do we integrate the two into identities anchored in the landscape? How do we assess resilience and the ability to be productive in the landscape? What is the role of new assessment approaches such as portfolios and digital footprints?

Creating imaginative spaces to support bridging boundaries

If curricula are to support students in engaging across boundaries, this requires new pedagogic approaches. In considering how to support students more effectively in using boundaries as sites of learning we have begun to consider ways in which we might extend our own practices as educators. How might we, for example, bridge between academic learning, informal learning, and workplace practice? One focus of attention has been writing practices. Often writing is a primary tool for reflection as a means to integrating workplace and academic learning (Bolton, 2005; Boud et al., 1985). Typically the link between practice and coursework is brought to life through writing assignments that involve structured reflection on a practice episode.

Usually students are required to write within academic conventions, to reference appropriate sources, and engage in detached analysis. They may be asked to relate a practice episode to a competence framework and explain how their actions demonstrate certain competencies or relate the episode to the learning outcomes of their course. Similarly in collaborative reflection with other students, or perhaps with a mentor or tutor, a piece of writing is often the starting point for creating a dialogue between theory and practice and between different student perspectives (e.g. Fenton-O'Creevy et al., 2006).

While such modes of writing have an important place, they can miss vital opportunities for learning. Consider these practice episodes: a novice nurse encounters a screaming baby covered in blood; an aspiring social worker comes face to face with a drunken client who threatens violence then collapses sobbing; a junior manager begins to realize that the project she has been assigned is failing and has to make a presentation to the senior team; a student teacher is hit by an egg as he turns his back in class. All have the potential to lead to considerable personal learning and development, but a detached academic account may lose much of the authentic experience of living through the episode, including the emotional and visceral quality of the experience. Consequently, much of the learning may be lost in attempts to shoehorn the experience into a particular academic writing genre and a set of pre-defined competencies or learning outcomes (Creme, 2003, 2005).

Useful approaches can involve encouraging learners to experiment with different writing genres and different modes of expression. Three interesting examples include:

- **Creative writing.** Besides acquisition of the skills involved, creative writing encompasses modes of reflection and imagination. Creative writing can particularly contribute a repertoire of techniques for 'freeing' writing: playing with roles, impersonation, putting on voices, a different outlook on the self, and individual behavior; all are textual tactics that can help 'interrogate' experience. Strategies used in life writing, in particular, demonstrate how we can use writing not only to 'capture' reality but to 'construct' it imaginatively.[3]

- **Academic literacies.**[4] One way to describe the field of academic literacies is to consider genres as dynamic reflections of landscapes of practice. A student practising academic literacies is encouraged to be reflective in switching between writing styles and genres, between one setting and another in the landscape. To use genres critically is to handle the social meaning and identities that each of those settings evokes. In an academic literacies development programme by Kings College London, for example, students from linguistic minority backgrounds who would like to study at university are taken explicitly through a process of reflecting on the way genres/modes vary across disciplines/subjects/fields, the distinctive features of each one, and the fluid overlap of the boundaries between them (Lee & Street, 2006).
- **Multimodal literacies.**[5] This approach encourages students to experiment with using more than one mode of communication. Genres of film, audio, photography, graphics, theatre, and speeches are seen as spaces for meaning-making and critical reflection. Reflecting on the meaning potential of different modes for different audiences across the landscape, students become aware of their own locations. They become strategic about crossing boundaries through multimodal texts that are more or less effective in different locations of that landscape.

Students of 'English for Specific Purposes' at a business school in Portugal[6] were assessed on their performance in presenting a business plan to an international investor looking for entrepreneurial business ideas in the local region. Throughout the semester they prepared both their business plan and their persona as players in a growing international market in Portugal. Their final assessment was based on a panel display and oral presentation. The instructor invited potentially interested local and international people (including, for example, the *Financial Times* reporter on Portugal) to attend and comment on how convincing each of the projects was. Not only did students have to learn to use business language and syntax in the service of presenting a convincing project but they were also invited to investigate and play with the kind of international identity they wanted to cultivate – such as deciding whether they wanted to use English or American spelling and expressions or whether they wanted to take on a more casual or more formal style (Mavor and Trayner, 2001).

As we have noted throughout the book, much work in developing professional competence and knowledgeability and in learning across boundaries is identity work. Developing a strong sense of personal and professional identity is a vital part of professional development. These approaches offer the opportunity to engage playfully with issues of identity and alignment with different parts of the landscape, providing a valuable space for reflection and development.

What creative spaces can we open up for learners to provide opportunities for acts of imagination that bridge across landscapes of practice? What kind of critical and reflective activities would extend learners' thinking in support of knowledgeability and identity work?

Universities in landscapes of practice

There is considerable public debate about the evolving place of universities in society. With tremendous changes in the degree of interconnectedness and opportunities for informal learning, and with the accelerating pace of change in the nature of work, many have questioned whether current models of higher education are fit for the future.

Universities should come to play a convening role across complex landscapes of practice; not simply producing or transmitting knowledge but convening the co-construction of new forms of knowledge, new practices, and social change.

Building on emerging practices

There is considerable potential in many of the explorations that are currently happening in higher education to build convening approaches. The Unconference movement attempts to shake the traditional format of academic conferences to encourage self-organizing enquiries. The 'connectivist' approach to MOOCs (Siemens, 2013) places the focus on learning through generating connections across networks. This is in contrast to what has been labelled the x-MOOC approach which mostly replicates classroom practices and pedagogies at scale on the internet (Daniel, 2012). Whilst the connectivist approach underplays the situated nature of knowledge and the difficulties of working across boundaries,[7] these approaches do suggest an appetite for new ways of connecting across landscapes of practice. By recognizing the potential for c-MOOCs and Unconferences as acts of convening across landscapes of practice and explicitly developing the necessary cross-boundary convening practices, we can significantly increase their potential for generating system-wide change and learning.

Towards an engaged scholarship

One of the disappointments of the Habiforum projects described in Chapter 7 was the failure of the academic and practitioner strands of work to build any real connection. All too easily academic practices can mitigate against real engagement with practice communities. Work on modes of 'engaged scholarship' by scholars such as Van de Ven (2007) champions approaches to social research that engage a wide range of stakeholders in defining and addressing problems. This could have important implications for how universities conduct research and scholarship. For example, a recent report to the UK research councils on innovation in technology-enhanced learning stresses the role of such engaged scholarship in generating educational innovations that have genuine impacts on practice (Scanlon et al., 2013).

> The University of Brighton in the UK has made the creation of strong university–community partnerships a centerpiece of its strategy. For instance, the project on resilience for children with special needs has taken to heart the role of the university as a legitimate convener of new spaces for learning across practices, including academic research, policy-making, service providers, parents, and youths (Hart and Wolf, 2006).

If we reimagine ourselves as systems conveners, what interventions might we make to reconfigure the landscape and create unique locations and encounters where multiple voices from academic and other practices can negotiate their boundaries productively?

What might it mean to abandon a view of universities as standing above the landscape and for them to play a convening role, co-constructing knowledge with practitioners from across landscapes of practice?

Notes

1. Much attention has been paid to the formation of professional identities (e.g. Ibarra, 1999; Lomax, 2013) and to educational institutions as spaces for identity work (e.g. Gallacher et al., 2002; Petriglieri & Petriglieri, 2010; Solomon, 2007; Wojecki, 2007).
2. See, for instance, Pegg et al. (2012); Yorke and Knight (2004).
3. We are grateful to Lindsay Anderson for these points
4. Academic Literacies build on New Literacy Studies, cf., Barton (1994); Gee (1996); Street (1984, 1995). An academic literacies approach treats reading and writing as social practices that vary with context, culture, and genre (Barton & Hamilton, 1998; Street, 1984, 1995). It is similar in many ways to the academic socialization model – or the apprenticeship trajectory from the periphery to the heart of the community – except that it views the processes as more complex and dynamic and includes power relations among people, communities, and institutions. It does not view literacy practices as being embedded solely in disciplinary and subject-based communities, but also examines how literacy practices from other institutions, such as business or government, are implicated in what students need to learn or do (Lee and Street, 2006).
5. Work on multimodal literacies and genre (Kress, 2003; Kress & Street, 2006; Van Dijk, 1997) emphasizes that communication involves all forms of its representation, including linguistic, actional, and visual. In the same way as academic literacies switch between genres, multimodal literacies involve switching between modes that are differently organized and established.
6. Escola Superior de Ciências Empresarias, Instituto Politécnico de Setúbal, Portugal.
7. Siemens (one of the co-founders of the Connectivist movement) often uses a tacit pipes metaphor in describing the movement of knowledge around a network. For example he describes the core idea of connectivist approaches to learning being 'that knowledge is distributed and learning is the process of navigating, growing and pruning connections' (Siemens, 2013: 12). This underplays the situated nature of knowledge and the varied identifications and accountabilities to different practices that will be represented in any convening process.

References

Allen, I. E. & Seaman, J. (2013). *Changing Course: Ten Years of Tracking Online Education in the United States.* Retrieved from http://files.eric.ed.gov/fulltext/ED541571.pdf (accessed 20 October 2013).

Barton, D. (1994). *Literacy: An Introduction to the Ecology of Written Language.* Oxford, UK: Blackwell.

Barton, D. & Hamilton, M. (1998). *Local Literacies.* London: Routledge.

Bolton, G. E. J. (2005). *Reflective Practice: Writing and Professional Development.* London: Sage Publications.

Boud, D. & Falchikov, N. (2007). *Rethinking Assessment in Higher Education: Learning for the Longer Term.* Abingdon: Routledge.

Boud, D., Keogh, R., & Walker, D. (Eds) (1985). *Reflection: Turning Reflection into Learning.* London: Kogan Press.

Creme, P. (2003). Why can't we allow students to be more creative? *Teaching in Higher Education, 8*(2), 237–277.

Creme, P. (2005). Should student learning journals be assessed? *Assessment and Evaluation in Higher Education, 30*(3), 287–296.

Daniel, J. (2012). Making sense of MOOCs: musings in a maze of myth, paradox and possibility. *Journal of Interactive Media in Education, 3.*

Fenton-O'Creevy, M., Knight, P., & Margolis, J. (2006). A practice-centered approach to management education. *New Visions of Graduate Management Education, 107,* 107–128.

Gallacher, J., Crossan, B., Field, J., & Merrill, B. (2002). Learning careers and the social space: exploring the fragile identities of adult returners in the new further education. *International Journal of Lifelong Education, 21*(6), 493–509.

Gee, J. P. (1996). *Social Linguistics and Literacies: Ideology in Discourse.* London: Falmer.

Hart, A. and Wolff, D. (2006). Developing local 'communities of practice' through local community–university partnerships. *Planning, Practice & Research, 21*(1), 121–138.

Ibarra, H. (1999). Provisional selves: experimenting with image and identity in professional adaptation. *Administrative Science Quarterly, 44*(4), 764–791.

Kress, G. (2003). *Literacy in the New Media Age.* London: Routledge.

Kress, G. & Street, B. (2006). Multi-modality and literacy practices. In K. Pahl & J. Rowsell (Eds), *Travel Notes from the New Literacy Studies.* Bristol, UK: Multilingual Matters.

Lea, M. R. & Street, B. V. (2006). The 'academic literacies' model: theory and applications. *Theory into Practice, 45*(4), 368–377.

Lomax, H. (2013). Managing identities. In S. MacKian & J. Simons (Eds), *Leading, Managing, Caring: Understanding Leadership and Management in Health and Social Care.* Oxford: Routledge.

Mavor S. & Trayner, B. (1991). Aligning genre and practice with learning in Higher Education: an interdisciplinary perspective for course design and teaching. *English for Specific Purposes,* (20), 345–366, Elsevier Science.

Pegg, A., Waldock, J., Hendy-Isaac, S., & Lawton, R. (2012). *Pedagogy for Employability.* York: Higher Education Academy.

Petriglieri, G. & Petriglieri, J. L. (2010). Identity workspaces: the case of business schools. *Academy of Management Learning & Education, 9*(1), 44–60.

Scanlon, E., Sharples, M., Fenton-O'Creevy, M., Fleck, J., Cooban, C., Ferguson, R., Waterhouse, P. et al. (2013). *Beyond Prototypes: Supporting Effective Research on Technology-enhanced Learning.* Milton Keynes, UK: Open University.

Siemens, G. (2013). Massive open online courses: innovation in education? In R. McGreal, W. Kinuthia & S. Marshall (Eds), *Open Educational Resources: Innovation, Research and Practice* (pp. 5–16). Athabasca: CO, Athabasca University.

Solomon, Y. (2007). Not belonging? What makes a functional learner identity in undergraduate mathematics? *Studies in Higher Education, 32*(1), 79–96.

Street, B. V. (1984). *Literacy in Theory and Practice.* Cambridge, UK: Cambridge University Press.

Street, B. V. (1995). *Social Literacies: Critical Approaches to Literacy Development, Ethnography and Education.* London: Longman.

Van de Ven, A. H. (2007). *Engaged Scholarship: A Guide for Organizational and Social Research.* Oxford: Oxford University Press.

Van Dijk, T. (Ed) (1997). *Discourse as Structure and Process.* London: Sage.

Wojecki, A. (2007). 'What's identity got to do with it, anyway?' Constructing adult learner identities in the workplace. *Studies in the Education of Adults, 39*(2), 168–182.

Yorke, M. & Knight, P. (2004). *Embedding Employability into the Curriculum* (Vol. 3). York: Learning and Teaching Support Network.

Index

Made in United States
Troutdale, OR
09/13/2023

12893413R00106